T0210047

I Seem to REMEMBER

Tyrus (Ty) Raymond Cobb, Jr.

I SEEM TO REMEMBER

iUniverse books may be ordered through booksellers or by contacting:

iUniverse
1663 Liberty Drive
Bloomington, IN 47403
www.iuniverse.com
844-349-9409

Because of the dynamic nature of the Internet, any web addresses or links contained in this book may have changed since publication and may no longer be valid. The views expressed in this work are solely those of the author and do not necessarily reflect the views of the publisher, and the publisher hereby disclaims any responsibility for them.

Any people depicted in stock imagery provided by Getty Images are models, and such images are being used for illustrative purposes only. Certain stock imagery © Getty Images.

ISBN: 978-1-6632-2866-6 (sc)
ISBN: 978-1-6632-2865-9 (e)

Library of Congress Control Number: 2021918478

Print information available on the last page.

iUniverse rev. date: 10/15/2021

CONTENTS

P-R-E-F-A-C-E

When I really "get goin'," things seem to fly out of this old brain with which the Lord provided me. I seem to be pondering the whatever and suddenly something comes to mind that "fancies" my tickle and I think of details of "something" that seems uncanny. Why just the other day the name of Mr. W. L. Sawyer of Claremore, OK, came to my mind, and now I will later write quite a bit of that nice man. More than a few people say, "How do you remember all that?" Sometimes it is really strange; (or maybe it is not?); sometimes about things occurred when I was 1 or 2 years old! Guess I should just start writing happenings and sort them 6 months from now. Maybe grandson can be my editor!!

(A little thing I must insert about my memory. I suffered a stroke in October 2015. Thankful to Beverly and the Lord, I was not left a cripple but I do have some lingering problems. My brain seems to have "canceled out some little cells of facts" such as peoples' names. So, as I write I will have to struggle to recover those facts. Hopefully that will also help me rebuilt those "damaged cells." Often I will have to think real "hard" to "recover" "lost" facts from my memory and I will not always be able to remember. When successful, I will be conducting successful self-therapy. Bear with me and have Oklahoma fun! ☺)

By the way. Beware, as I write sort of "folksy." The reader will find a lot of information about how things were "back when" in general.

Surely you will find what I have passed to the reader interesting, informative by the "ages" when things happened, and most of all . . . humorous. Read, smile, and enjoy, hundreds of snippets about growing up in Oklahoma!

FAMILY STUFF

Where have I resided when these happenings occurred?

Start in Duncan, OK on 23 June 1940 with the handsome (yucky) newborn son of Tyrus R. Cobb (born in Foss, OK in 1913) and his lady, Mary E. Bagby Cobb (born in Olmstead, IL in 1919) – me, Tyrus Raymond Cobb, Jr. By the way, I think the doctor who birthed me was D. Patterson who doctored in a 2 or 3 floor tannish-yellow brick building hospital in Duncan that was about three times bigger than my current home. That building was to be named the Patterson Hospital and was still there about 12 years ago; today, I know what.

My father graduated from the Oklahoma Highway Patrol (OHP) "academy" with the first ever graduating class in 1936. Remember seeing pictures of my father astride an OHP motorcycle. Believe he was first "stationed" in Claremore, OK in 1937, and shortly was moved from there to Duncan where he met and courted my mother, Mary. Guess she was impressed with that man in a uniform as she fell in love, got married and made me! Thank you very much !

Generally, things started happening when we moved from Duncan (1005 ½ Oak, 1941) to Chickasha, OK for the OHP. WW II came and my father left the OHP (after 6 1/2 years) to be a guard and fireman at an oil refinery back in Duncan in support of the war. Fortunately, my father was a jack-of-all-trades and was able to secure work after the war, as the refinery job was not so good (may have gotten laid off).

I remember finding myself traveling back to Patterson Hospital while we lived there. When five, I had my tonsils removed . . . I remember the nurse or doctor saying "listen for the airplane taking off" (me crying when they placed the ether mask over my face). Remember my throat being sore, and I was told that as soon as I could eat a dill pickle I was cured. Doctor visited at home (715 E. Pine Street) . . . yeah, doctors really did execute home visits for patients. I remember Dr. Patterson's black doctor's bag containing his instruments and medicines.

I visited Patterson Hospital again near Easter of 1949 when I had my appendix removed (it was within an hour of "bursting" which could have been fatal). I remember that dad had my appendix (looked like a shrimp) in a little glass (looked like a whiskey jigger) that we keep in the house on a shelf in dad's bedroom – think we kept it for at least a year – ugh!

My scar was kept closed by three metal clamps that held the skin together and required me to bend over to the right because the clamps pulled the skin together. Remember my Aunt Bea (not Opry's aunt Bea!!) came to see me and bought me a gold mesh bag full of "gold coins," at least I thought they were real gold. I was rich ! ! Just chocolate candy with gold aluminum.

After about five or six days in the hospital, I went home (now living on 1408 Elder Street in Duncan in a small, new house that dad had had built – more on that later). Someone brought me a bag of candy Easter sugar eggs. I ate too many of them and I vomited all over the place; they thought that I would have to go back to the hospital - - I was really "sick". I survived.

Enough about Dr. Patterson (folks loved him; me too!) and my visits with him.

At this point, I want to lay out where the family lived in some detail then tell of things and stuff.

Born in Duncan; moved to Chickasha on or about Jun 1942; Alvin Bruce (2nd son) born in Chickasha (Jul 1943) (he was not as pretty as I !!); moved to Duncan to take oil refinery job/other jobs (Teddy Ney, #3, born Oct 1947); moved back to Chickasha in Nov 1951 (East 7th Street); moved to Claremore in Aug 1954 (parents remained here for life); Ty, Jr. (me) went to USMA until 6 Jun 1962 (married to Beverly J. York on 7 Jun 1962; still "hanging"); Army schools at Ft Benning, GA 1962-1963); Ft Campbell, KY until c. Feb 1965); Korea 1965-1966; Ft Benning 1966-1967; Vietnam 1967-68; Austin, TX Dec 68 to May 70); West Point 1970-1973; I was assigned to Korea and family remained at Steward AFB 1973-74; Ft Benning 1974-1978; Picatinny Arsenal 1978-1983; Sparta, NJ 1978-2005; and here we sit in Salisbury, NC in May 2005 to today in 2021.

Yes, we moved a lot of times, and we had many "side-trips" during major moves, e.g., three different homes while stationed at Ft Campbell and a three week SECRET Nuclear Weapons Employment course at Ft Benning before first, one year, unaccompanied tour in South Korea.

Now we will visit the Tyrus R. Cobbs, Jr. as they move around and live.

The Law is Here!
Dad is in middle and
me "leading" c. late 1941

Me in Duncan, OK age 6 months

Grandma Cobb with me in
Elk City, OK 1940

Mom and Dad with me wearing
Mom's OHP "creation" c. 1942

My 1st Christmas 1940

REAL EARLY CHICKASHA

In pictures, I have seen myself walking a leashed young black puppy on a sidewalk. I appear to be about 2 years old (1942), and this must be in Chickasha after we had moved a year ago from Duncan. My earliest memory is talk about an animal had escaped from the city zoo; it seems to have been a bear or monkey. Whatever, the animal had a furry coat. There were several trucks (construction??) that parked in a "yard" next to our apartment. I "saw" something that stuck fur out from the truck yard. A real sighting or a figment of a 2-year old's imagination?? Probably the latter, but I remember an animal escaping. Escape would have been from the Shannon Springs Park (more later) where animals were caged (not well caged by today's standards).

Things get a bit fuzzy about Chickasha but for the above incident, though many pictures "tell" us a lot about the little Cobb family. Tommy Riley sticks in my mind as he was a chum of mine from pictures, as well of the picture of me in the little highway patrol "uniform" my mother made for me. My picture in the uniform (in my possession) also made a copy into the Duncan paper, me standing in front of three troopers, Cullen Riley, my dad and another unknown trooper. (God, I was cute! Thanks mom; she always was very handy with a sewing machine.)

COBBS RESIDE IN DUNCAN

Shortly after Bruce was born, dad left the Patrol and took a defense job as a guard and fireman (c. Oct 1943) at a small oil refinery in Duncan. He was scheduled to get called up for the service, (World War II was now seen in almost every aspect of Americans' endeavor; later more on the impact of Americans' everyday life, especially the young Cobbs) but as he was now father of two children and worked in a defense job, he was deferred. (Both of dad's brothers, James Irwin [oldest of 3 Horace Dixon, Sr. and Pearl Cobb's sons] who everybody called "Ty," and Horace, youngest of the sons saw service in the military in WW II.) J. I. was in the Navy and Horace, stationed in Europe; was in Army Air Corps as a glider pilot. He used to kid all us kids by telling us that he had killed Hitler!

Now four years old in Duncan, I started getting vivid remembrances I still have.

Me in a Patriotic uniform during WWII c. 1943.

War Ration Book One issued for Ty Cobb, Jr.
May 6, 1942

MAIN STREET

As I remember, we lived in four different abodes from 1943 through 1950 and I remember them all. The first was a house (300 block of East Main) sitting on a hill about two blocks from Duncan's downtown business sector. There was a slope down toward business district from our house; was probably a small stream about halfway between us and the business district. One block from the stream was a big garage for vehicle repairs. The road that ran in front of our house ran east of town; our house was on the north side of road. (This road ran east of town and to a friend of family about a mile from town - - more about the family later.)

Here it comes . . . ! The "neatest" thing about the house was it had a four-inch hole in the middle of kitchen floor. We occasionally took looks to see what was going on under the house! There's more. I remember swallowing some coins (nickel and two pennies). Tummy hurt; called the doctor; Dr. Patterson said collect all of Ty, Jr's poop, check through it and count to seven cents; Ty, Jr. is cured! I used to sit on the porch and watch downhill toward town as Daddy always came from that direction after work.

In those days, the "have-nots" were said to live on the "wrong" side of the tracks. And that is where we lived, but we were okay. Nearly every small-to-medium sized -town/city in America had at least one railroad that ran right through the middle of town, thus two sides. This house, "on the wrong side of the tracks," was where we were, and we did not hurt a bit; there was love in the house! Family, hard-working Dad and home boss Mom with two youngsters.

Mom had me don an Army formal uniform and had my picture taken by a professional photographer (still have the large photo). Seems a lot of folks had their kids' pictures taken in military uniforms as a patriotic move.

I had one brilliant event that I have drilled into my head. It may have been V-Day in Europe, but more likely V-Day in the Pacific (Japan). Suzanne Holcomb (teenaged daughter of Ted and Bea Holcomb; Bea was sister of my mother's father, Harry Ney Bagby; thus, Mom's Aunt Bea) was my second cousin. Suzanne took me downtown for the celebration for Victory. Duncan's main street was absolutely mobbed with all kinds of noise of a hundred ways. I thought it was cool, but "noisy." Everyone was very happy.

Suzanne also took me to a Sunday church service, think it was the First Christian Church in Duncan. She probably wanted me with her to get attention from her friends. At that time I was five and she must have been about 14-16. Must have been a thing for "cute" young kids to accompany teenagers at that time (I wasn't Chuck Berry but I loved the man's music). I remember that the folks even served me/us with grape juice! Much later, I learned that was my first communion.

Uncle Ted's family lived in Duncan, and he owned the Ford

dealership there. I remember Aunt Bea's home (on the "right side of the tracks"). Later you will see that we moved to within a couple of blocks from her, but not a house nearly as big. I remember Bea had a real "nice" laundry, she had a "side-by-side" washer (with glass door) and dryer (few had such; we certainly did not). I used to get a kick out of watching clothes and soap suds spinning around sort of like watching TV. Of course, at that time I did not know what TV was! Aunt Bea used to carefully step onto an unfinished storage area to pull out Ted, Jr. toy cars (about 19-20 then). Not sure what he was doing at that time, maybe college, as I did not see him much. He was a nice, handsome young man. Actually, the entire family was nice, handsome folks.

Let's move on.

PINE STREET

Someone, I assume in Duncan, foresaw a need for rent houses and apartments, especially with the service men and women "coming home" as the end of the war in Europe looked nearly over. Anyway someone built four or five single houses and a bunch of apartments, usually four apartments each to about ten buildings. All buildings and the single houses were completely bricked with dark tan bricks.

We moved into one of the brand new single rent houses on Pine Street; now we were on the "right side of the tracks" but only by about a block! I remember a lot of events that took place there, such as when I had my tonsils removed and Dr. Patterson's visits.

We had a large tree in the front yard and we used to dig "roads and tunnels" among its large roots and "drove our cars in that maze." We had a beautiful collie male dog who "adopted" us for a couple of months; true owner finally found and took the collie back home. At one time we had another small dog, probably a cocker spaniel.

The apartment area (several four-apartments-per-building) next to our house was well laid out with drainage ditches (well-sloped about four feet wide and a foot deep with nice Bermuda grass growing throughout). The edges of the ditches had hedges about three feet high growing next to the ditches. There was a cut in the hedges as another ditch ran perpendicular to the main ditch. Also there was a single strand of tight barbed wire strung through the hedges about a foot off the ground; that made the wire two feet high as it went over the one foot drainage ditch. The trap was set!

My uncle Horace and his wife, Jerry, came to visit and, of course, brought our cousins, Gary (about 9) and Jimmy (about 7). Gary took a liking to our dog and he asked if he could walk him on a lease. Sure. He took off into the apartments' area. As dogs would, the dog wanted to run. Off he went almost dragging Gary running behind. The dog ran under the wire in the drainage ditch; Gary did not see the single strand of barbed wire. He ran into that barbed wire going full blast. We heard the screaming as we all went running to find Gary down with nasty cuts on both legs. (I cringe now just thinking of Gary as he collided with that barbed wire. Still "feel" it and that was seventy-five years ago!)

Marvin and Vanilla, the Brumetts, lived across the street from us in the same type house; their kids were Marla (4) and Jay (2). We kids' ages were made for playmates. At the time, polio was on the rampage throughout America, so naturally parents were careful to "manage" their youngsters the way doctors so-guided parents. "Experts" thought polio had some connection with afternoon sun and swimming in the mid-afternoon. So, no swimming until 4 PM and take a nap after lunch every day.

Vanilla and my mom took their kids to kiddy pools at Duncan Park after 4 PM. The pool was covered with shade by the numerous trees near the pool. We loved it. Moms also demanded naps about 1 PM every day. One day Marla and I were laid together on a bed to "sleep" for the afternoon. Somehow the two of us got to talking about how we were different in our pants. Oh, really? Yeah. Let's check. Not sure which of us pushed this conversation, but to protect Marla, I will be chivalrous and say I "started" it. We proceeded and "it was no big thing" and she was a "blank". And then Mom walked in, scolded us and told us to stop. At that age (4 and 5), "it" truly was no big thing!

AIR CONDITIONING ?

In those days, there was really no such thing as air-conditioning. Therefore, we lived with the windows wide open praying for a relieving breeze, but it usually did not help much. Folks, in Oklahoma the summer days' temperature was normally around 105 degrees. We used electric fans to help. At night we slept in our boxers (underwear) and splashed water onto our chests and laid in front of the fan. Worked for about 4 minutes!

My Dad was always handy with his hands and had been good at high school "shop" courses. He built a water-cooled air conditioner. It was a "box" to fit into the bottom half of a window. The box sides had two sheets of galvanized wire with ½ inch grid openings. About two inches between the two sheets of wire, Dad stuffed excelsior (looks spaghetti like made out of wood) into the two sheets of wire; above that he attached a copper tube with small holes that would drip water down through excelsior. The water was from an outside faucet attached to the copper tube. Then an electric fan was placed into the box. With water and the fan on, outside air was drawn through the excelsior cooling the outside air into the house. It cooled at least one room; usually Dad/Mom's bedroom.

One night Mom and Dad had gone to the movies or something, so they got a babysitter for Bruce and me; she was a teenager about 16 years old. We were laying on Mom's bed with the window raised to the top and the adjacent window with Dad's air-conditioner, as she read a story to us. Suddenly, someone's fist was raised in the open window and the person said something like "We are gotten get you!" We were really scared. The sitter called the police and they were here pretty quickly; they looked around and found nothing and left. We shut the window!

Next to the Brummett's house was another house (not in the apartment complex) to the right as we faced their house. The man in the house was about 50 years old and liked to kid around with the kids. One day we all were watching several dogs as they romped around, and someone raised the question of why dogs kept smelling each others' butts. The fellow "took the lead" explaining why the dogs smell each others' butts. Seems many, many years ago all the dogs held a huge "dog get-together." During the "party" some of the dogs stole all the ice cream. Today, now dogs are looking to find out who ate all the ice cream!

During War II, there were almost no automobiles being made, as all such manufacturing was used to make jeeps, truck and tanks. Somehow Dad got hold of an older Ford vehicle by taking the rumble seat out of the back and there built in a pick-up bed. Of course, the "new" model-T was black.

ORIGINAL OLEO

I do remember a few things about what went on at the home front during WW II. Mom had war ration books and I remember her saying once, "I have enough rations to get some gas." I also remember that butter was almost impossible to get, so we improvised. We could buy "imagination butter" that was white and looked like shortening. With the purchase we got a small envelope of red powder and then mixed it into the "white stuff" to make it yellow. I have no idea what it was, but it was "okay." Hey, the war's on! Learn to live it! (That stuff became oleo!!)

Different organizations were always going around collecting scarce items. People would collect about anything that was metal. I remember doing my part. We used to strip "tin foil" from our gum wrappers. Never got a medal but we were proud to contribute.

Dad always liked to go fishing, so one day he took me about 4 miles to Lake Duncan to fish with him. I did catch a fish but when the fish struck the line I ran up the bank in fright! What a fishing man! Dad calmed me down, and I pulled in the one foot bass. With Dad's help, of course. When we got home we told Mom, and all wanted to take a picture of me and my fish. There I was on the back porch holding up the fish with a six inch piece of wire in the fish's mouth, so I would not have to touch it!

Shortly after we moved to Pine Street, a couple built a neighbor grocery store on the corner across the street a half block from our house. The store was on a well-travelled city street, so we were not allowed to cross that street without supervision. Good idea and it also kept us from begging for a penny or two to visit the store for penny candy.

Everybody knows how hot, not warm, hot it can be in Oklahoma, so we all looked forward to getting something cold to eat. Our folks could buy us ice cream or they could make some with an ice cream, hand-crank machine. That was the best! After Mom made the batch with all that ice cream stuff mixins', she married that together with a lot of milk; Dad put it in the medal cylinder in a wooden vat with ice and a bit of rock salt and cranked away for about thirty minutes. Dad would sometimes put peppermint candy sticks in the batch and boy, oh boy was that good!

Store-bought cold items for individuals were popsicles and fudgsicles. My favorite popsicle flavor was cherry. We would be seen trying to make our own popsicles in the 4-ice tray little freezing compartment of our frig, but they were never as good as store-brought ones.

OUR DAD, THE HERO

Dad had been a firefighter when he lived in Elk City, OK, before he married Mom. All his life if he was not an official fireman, he liked to be around other firemen. When we lived in Duncan, he had been a volunteer fireman. I think he got about two or three dollars for each time he aided official firemen at fires. I remember there were quite a few grass fires that he attended.

Then, a <u>really big fire</u> started on a few freight cars on the railroad track about two blocks from our house. Dad saw it start and Mom begged him not to go. But, I guess fighting fire was in his blood. Off he went. When fighting the fire for about an hour, someone noticed a large truck afire, next to the tracks and under a large fuel tank. All felt the fire would cause the fuel tank to explode and cause major damage and possibly deaths. Dad did not hesitate. He ran and jumped into the truck (the bed now aflame) and drove the truck well away from the fuel tank, parked the truck, then ran from the truck. Guess my dad was a hero. It took firemen another three hours to completely extinguish the fire.

Marla and Jay's grandparents lived a couple of blocks from us. They were J. G. and Effie Brummett and J. G. was a judge. His son was Marvin, Marla's father. He too was a lawyer and worked in the corporate headquarters of Halliburton, an oil field equipment and expertise enterprise, with the original company headquarters in Duncan. With the thirst for oil to fuel America's economy, Halliburton grew at warp speed to eventually be headed in Dallas and had business all over the world, especially the Middle East. Marvin was a tall handsome man and was a great dad to Marla and Jay. . . .and a friend to the Cobbs for years. I remember riding (c. 1945) to Chickasha and back to Duncan on Halliburton's corporate plane (probably a joy ride; Dad loved airplanes.) Dad showed me how the bathroom emptied its waste; that's right folks, right out bottom of the plane! We got a great kick looking at the Earth by looking out the bottom of the "modern" toilet! Hope, "that" did not hit anyone. (Fortunately, today's aircraft designers have corrected that flaw.)

My Dad could do just about anything and did. I learned that Dad was a licensed airplane pilot for small craft. I remember seeing a couple of pictures of Dad with a couple of other guys at the airport (Chickasha

I think) before I was born. Those and Dad owned a small aircraft there. Unfortunately, one to the other guys had a crash when he was landing and ended up upside down probably by a heavy wind. Ended that craft!

Then when I was about six or seven, Dad again showed up with a nice small aircraft in Duncan. I even "helped" build the hangar for the plane at the Duncan airport. Remember the hangar with 2" x 4" lumber which constituted the frame to which sheets of tin were hammered onto the wood frame. Dad liked to hang around with flyers and mechanics at the airport and several times took me with him. He even took me up in his plane once, when there had been a train wreck and we circled it for a while. I was glad to get back on ground, as I was not too confident of how sturdy the plane was . . . thought I might "fall through the bottom!" In those days the skin of light aircraft was basically made out of light canvas to keep weight low. (Today, skin of even light aircraft is made of thin sheet aluminum.)

Dad always kept his license to fly up to date and I believe his still had it into his sixties.

Back to J.G. and Effie (probably aged in late 50s or early 60s). We used to play at their house and Effie seemed to love having the kids there. J. G. had a rather large playhouse built that we played in in their backyard. I remember sitting in a breakfast nook off Effie's kitchen that was new to us and was neat in which to eat there. Later, I walked by their house on the way (about four blocks) to school at Emerson school in second grade. Nice folks.

NO "COLONEL SANDERS" CHICKEN HERE

How did fried chicken make its way to the dinner table? "He/she" did not take a taxi there! He showed up alive with all of his feathers intact. I do not remember Mom "undressing" the chicken. But, the lady next door certainly knew how. I watched her several times grab a chicken by the neck and pull its head off, then throw the poor chicken out on the lawn to jump and squam in its death dance with blood flying around. Then she dipped the chicken in hot water to help the chicken divest itself of its feathers, with a little pulling. All loved the fried chicken. Man, what would the World do without chickens!

By the way, Grandma Nina Bagby (Mom's mother) was the world's expert on preparing live (soon to be fried) chickens. Grandma and her husband (Harry Ney Bagby) raised beef cattle, chickens, cotton, and soy beans. Grandma not only prepared chickens for frying, but she raised them (about 25 at a time) from her own fertilized eggs, through chicks to grown chickens. Once grown, if you did not lay eggs in nests she built, you might find yourself gracing a plate on her table!

Bruce and I played about a zillion hours of cowboys and Indians, especially from the time we moved onto Pine Street. We always had a cowboy hat on and a six-shooter on our hip. Conversations might go . . . "Bang! Bang! I got you first." "No! You didn't." "Yes, I did." "No. You didn't. I dodged!" Argued and argued and argued the whole day long. Fortunately none of us were "killed!" And then along came "caps" (a teeny, teeny bit of gun powder impacted in a strip of red paper. Each of those "bits" made a loud sound when exploded by being struck in a toy cap pistol. Most toy guns would hold a roll of 50 caps.) Holy cool, buckaroo!

We used to watch movies where the bad guys and good guys would get into gun battles and never run out of bullets. Those were not six-shooters; they were "twenty-six shooters"! And we were just like in the movies. We had rolls of fifty caps, thus fifty shots. Then some guy invented real toy six-shooters. These toy guns had real cylinders that would only take a special flat circle of six "bits" of gun powder caps. So that means that a buckaroo "fired" six shots then he had to reload. That was also cool, but kids liked the rolls of fifty shots. (A thing that I really liked was to take a whole roll of fifty "bits," lay it on the pavement or concrete side-walk, and hit it hard with a hammer. That made a really loud sound. So, cool!)

Many youngsters had some form of wagon; usually they were made of metal. Ours was different, and I never saw, then or later, another like it. It was made of wood and had wooden side-boards. We used it like it was a "covered wagon." We even took it to a big event at the Duncan High School football stadium with the Cub Scouts. We pulled the wagon like it was a covered wagon and running from the "Indians". Cub Scouts were the cowboys and Indians. Such drama!

H. D. COBB, OUR GRANDPA

One day Grandpa Cobb (Horace Dixon) visited us, primarily to take Bruce and me to Elk City, OK where he and Grandma Cobb (Pearl) lived. Bruce and I were cleaned up and were sporting new leather beanies that Aunt Bea had given us because she thought they were cute. I guess we did too. Our names were burned onto the leather bream of the beanies: "Bruce" and "Ty Ty." I never liked that as my name, but after several years I "out grew it." The ride to Elk City was about a two hour ride.

The Grand-folk Cobbs were the official Federal government weather data recorders of that area. They recorded temperature, humidity, wind and moisture two or three times a day. We always thought that was cool.

Grandpa Cobb owned the Phillips 66 filling station on a main road (believe it or not it was on highway US66) through Elk City. We were in awe of a display in the station. It was a display board with pocket-knifes that we craved on and on and talked about them.

One day we were called for lunch and grandpa was there too. And, there they were . . . a new knife beside each of our plates! Man, we were awesome now! The next day we were doing our afternoon "nap," and got to comparing our knives. Oops! Either Bruce or I cut a finger. Yes, blood. We swore the cat had done it. We were not very good story tellers. How could they not believe us two cute little boys?

My Dad was working for Uncle Ted at his Ford agency as a mechanic after the job at the oil refinery. One day he was installing new lights in the ceiling of the shop on a long (about 25 feet) ladder. Another was supposed to be holding the ladder and he stoops for a minute. You guessed it . . . the ladder slid and Dad fell from the ladder and hit the concrete floor quite hard. He was worried but continued to work. The pain continued as Dad walked home from work (about 5 blocks). He had to stop and sit down a couple of times to seek relief from the pain. This was the beginning a four or five year medical saga. Basically, Dad worked with the pain for a long time before he got an operation on his back. We will re-visit Dad's painful times later.

All three Cobb boys went through several childhood diseases that came a calling to most of them when they hit the Pine Street abode. We had mumps, chicken pox, measles and German measles, the three day malady. Chicken pox left a tell-tail mark on us if we scratched the pox whelp. I remember Ted was still crawling when he got the pox and he used to rub his head and face on the carpet trying to relieve the itch. He got a few of the marks, a circular indention in one's skin about a 0.2 or 0.3 inch across. He had two or three tell-tail marks, and I got one that stayed with me for about twenty years.

Oklahoma experienced cold weather in January and February and those "winds came sweeping down the plains" could get nippy. Mom had the situation . . . we pulled our trousers over our pajamas' bottoms and we were ready to brave the cold winds. We also had a winter cap (usually a Christmas present) that was made of corduroy with ear flaps; we untied and pulled them over our ears.

UNCLE "TY"

Uncle "Ty" (actually James Irving) and his wife, Mary Eddie came from Benton, Arkansas for a visit at our Pine Street house in Duncan. Dad had built a little outside barbecue pit and he really cooked great steaks.

(Recipe for sauce: Ketch-up, 57 sauce, Worcestershire sauce, mustard, salt, pepper, and any other condiment lying around in the cabinet.) Dad cooked the steaks outside and they had lots of sauce covering the meat. We ate on paper plates, the thick ones that were like soft card board. Uncle Ty and Dad had a few beers and the feast was on. Eating, talking, scrapping, eating, drinking, talking, and so and. Some of the sauce was absorbed into the plate and fortunately Uncle Ty actually had mistaken picked up two plates when he got his steak. He continued eating until he was finished. When Mom went to pick up the plates she noticed that Uncle Ty had eaten a hole about three inches across of the top plate! Everybody roared! Mom kept the plate and when Uncle Ty left, Mom rinsed off the plate let it dry. Then, Dad put the "hole- in" plate into a package and mailed it to Uncle Ty.

Later, when I was about 10 and Bruce was 7 we traveled to Benton, Arkansas, where lived James Irving (Ty) Cobb (Dad's older brother). Uncle "Ty" was out of the Navy (WW II) and working for Reynolds Aluminum Company. I remember his daughter, Marilyn Jo, our cousin who was about 16 at that time. Again, teenager girls thought it was cool to "parade" little kids around to their friends. She took us to the swimming pool to parade us with her girl-friends. Did not mind that.

A couple of years later we went back to Benton and met Marilyn Jo's new husband (Ty Robinson) just out of the Marine Corps and was now working for Reynolds. Bruce and I felt he was cool because he could crush a tin (not aluminum) beer can with his hands. They had a new baby daughter, Adela Beth.

(Uncle J. I. "Ty" became one of the major corporate officials for the new Corpus Christi (Texas) Reynolds aluminum plant and they moved there. Marilyn Jo and her family also moved to Corpus and they and/ or their kin are in Corpus today.)

FIRST GRADE

In 1946 the people of the Catholic folks in Duncan got together and built a large building next to the Catholic Church which was one block from the Cobb house on Pine Street. The Catholics were thinking ahead because the new building had three or four classrooms in it. Their plan was to start with a first grade class and each year add the next class, second class, and a new class each year. Mom enrolled me in the first class in Duncan; I only went one year, as I guess the cost permitted no more classes there for me. (I did well in school the rest of my el-hi schooling and was valedictorian of my senior class in 1958. Did my attendance at the first grade at the Catholic school make a difference? Only God knows.)

I really took to girls in the first grade, though Marla was still "my girl" (I think) waiting to become a first grader next year. So I "looked around" the campus. Remember . . . I was really cute and the girls liked me! One cute girl took a liking to me (how could she resist!) and only lived across the street from the school and on the way to my home. I could actually walk through folks' yards and be home in three minutes. The girl's house had an unattached garage with a dirt "floor." She asked me to walk with her as I started home after school. We (do not know who suggested but) we went into the garage and sat together on a large wooden box. Before you know it, we were kissing! I liked it. Shortly, I heard Mom calling for me, so we broke it up. I do not know the girl's name, but we were friends.

I became an amateur actor, as I was a shepherd in the annual Christmas play in first grade. I sought for an Oscar, but it was not to be. I have a picture (8x10 glossy) of me and the cast, and looking at the picture recently, two girls' names came to my mind: Sarah Wilke and Linda Beth Patterson. I remember that Linda Beth who was about 2 or 3 inches taller than me, and invited me to her house to play. Her folks must have been a bit wealthy as their home was huge on a lot of about 2 or 3 acres and they had a large concrete wading pool in the yard. Both of these two girl friends are in the glossy picture sitting on the first row to right wearing crowns. Wonder if they are still alive! I pray so.

Me (1 1/2 years old) with Dad in Chickasha, OK

Ty Cobb Jr. 1st grade in Christmas play; shepherd with a sheep. (right of picture)

My teacher at the Catholic School was Sister Stanislaus. She was tall and big and I remember her big black leather belt the wrapped around her waist and the tongue of it hung also to the floor. Very intimidating! However, she was nice and I never heard of her spanking anyone. She was also the principal and there was one other Nun. This Nun was sort of our music teacher. At Christmas she was working to get us to recite the poem, "The Night Before Christmas." She had some kind of recording machine that cut our voices onto a 45 rpm record so that each student would have a record of our recitation to give to our parents. I made about eight lines and that was all I could remember, but my voice was recorded.

Second grade for me was at Emerson public school. Mrs. Odie, my teacher, was a short, roly-poly type and was nice. Mrs. Nunnley was our music teacher and I remember learning a lot of verses of Ole McDonald's Farm; she must have taught us well, as I can still sing most of them. (Want to hear some? Nah!)

About this time, attended Sunday School at the First Baptist Church and I still remember the lessons taught us. A vividly remember of an older (remember I was only seven) lady and what she wore. She wore a mink wrap over her Sunday suit. Why do I remember – her wrap was two dead and skinned minks and they were each biting each other's tail! This wrap had their eyes intact. Now a mink coat can be a beautiful thing, but this thing struck me as hideous.

Emerson School was heated with steam and the steam was produced by burning coal. I remember a pile of coal outside the basement door and later those pieces of coal were burned down to ash and materials in the coal that were not carbon minerals so they were just thrown out on the ground.

One of the kiddie books we had was "Little Black Sambo" who was the young boy who was the central character. We all thought he was a good guy and we wished we had him with whom to play. Our first introduction to Black people was a positive one. As we got older in our good family, we became of age knowing that all children were God's.

PENNIES FOR POLIO

A couple of events still cross my mind about second grade. The whole USA had an event for the March of Dimes to collect money for research to cure infantile paralysis (polio). We were given a card with 5 slots and asked to put a dime in each slot and turn in the card with the money. Everybody wanted to give, as polio was hanging over all of us at that time. However, I never saw too many with 5 dimes; most were maybe a nickel and four pennies. Thing was, everybody tried. (A cure, via a vaccine shot or swallowing a sugar cube with medicine in it, conquered polio around 1956. So, those dimes and nickels and pennies paid off! Thank you.)

The other event of my memory was the accident of the little girl who sat in front of me at Emerson School. Our desks were connected in a long line of say 7 desks. The little girl's seat back was connected to my desk top. She must have been afraid to ask to go to the restroom, so eventually she went on her seat then onto the floor by my feet. Hey, when you gotta go, you gotta go!

One of the games the boys at Emerson played at recess (we also played a lot at home) was "Punt and Rubbly." One guy kicks the ball and tries to make it go to the opponent's goal (line) without being touched (1 point). If one kicks a ball into air and his opponent catches it; he can take five steps toward his opponent's goal. When one steps across the opponent's goal, it is a touchdown (6 points). Confused? You are too old, you have to be young to understand!

Mom and Dad befriended a couple who lived on a farm about a mile east of Duncan who had a son, Jackie, about a year older than I. Jackie was a rough, tough farm boy who worked hard and was a great help to his mom and dad.

We used to go out just to visit and, of course, play. We used to run down a hill to their watering pond where their Hereford cattle watered there. Besides the cattle and naturally fish were the dreaded water moccasins! We threw rocks at them, but we did not get too close.

Jackie's folks (I do not remember their father's name, but the mother was Lallay) had a great vegetable garden. It grew all kinds of things in the garden that was about 100 x 50 yards. I was most impressed by potatoes because the foliage was a beautiful green and very lush about two feet tall. Of course, in the ground were the huge potatoes and we used to dig up a whole mess of them to take home.

I remember one Fourth of July we were at their house and set to watch an aerial show from a distance of two miles from the show. It was performed at about a thousand feet about the ground in Duncan. The dare devils were "wing walking" and later did a parachute jump. Folks, that was amazing in 1948! We bunch of Okies had never seen such. Today, it is seen often but still breath-taking.

One day Jackie came to our house on Elder Street to spend the night with us. We soon knew why he had never been to our house before. About midnight Jackie had an asthma seizure and his mom came and took him home. We shortly moved to Chickasha and never saw them again. (I would bet that the Duncan city limits is beyond Jackie's childhood home and has filled in that watering pond. Bye, bye snakes!)

While we lived on Pine Street, I remember Uncle Billy and a few of his workers (Americans) stopped one evening to eat and sleep at our house. One of the workers had worked for Uncle Bill for years and they were real buddies; he was J.R. Martin. I remember Uncle Bill took out a roll of US cash, about four thousand dollars and showed us. He and his workers drove there in a semi-trailer and tractor. That was the "rig" of the time for moving things (and people) around. Back then the rig was smaller than semi-trailers are today. The tractor (truck) had two front wheels and four (two duos) in the rear and a heavy tow hitch; the trailer had four (two duos) heavy wheels on the trailer. (Today's semi rigs would have at least 18 wheels). Uncle Bill was going to Mexico to get a load of Mexican workers to work his 640 acres in southeast Missouri.

A few years after World War II a lot of "tin" metal toys began to be seen in the market. There would be little cars, animals and such. We were told that this was how Japan was going to re-build their economy after the devastation of the Japan's bombing. They were making the toys out of scrap metal. They were going to build back their economy a dime at a time. Those folks have really come a long way by . . . hard work! (Today just look at their cars, machinery and electronic devices, computers and televisions. They are showing us a thing or two! Now it is the Chinese!)

DADDY AND I GO-A-BALING HAY

At the end of the War, farm equipment was still difficult to get because factories had been making war equipment for the last four years, and most had not yet re-tooled to farm equipment. Working with Uncle Ted, Dad made a deal to buy a new Ford so he could trade it for a New Holland hay baler and a Ford tractor. Since I do not remember of a single hay baler in the county, having one could help one make good money, if he was willing to work hard. Dad was ready to do that. So Dad went in the business of offering to bale a farmers' hay that had been cut, dried and wind-rowed. He had a circuit throughout the county to hit nearly every hay field about every two or three weeks. His Ford tractor pulled the baler around the county and onto hay fields. He truly worked from dawn to sunset; folks, that is 14 to15 hours a day during Oklahoma's summers.

That was good work, but there was a catch. Hay-growing season was normally only from April thru October. He then got a five month job as the town police radio operator and dispatcher. He was a natural, having been a fireman (in Elk City) and a State Trooper in Claremore, Duncan and Chickasha. One of the winters when he was not in the hay fields, he worked as a fleet mechanic for OK Transfer and Moving Company, Duncan. Mr. Max Holesberline owned the company with about half a dozen moving vans. He and his family lived about a block from us when living on Pine Street and I played a bit with his younger son. One of Dad's jobs was to convert all the trucks to a <u>new innovation</u>, turn signals. They were crude when compared to today's turning signals. They were just like mechanical arms that went up, straight out, or down imitating your arm movement signals. (Today, we would laugh at those things, but then they were state-of-the-art and required.)

Dad must have made better than good money in the baling business, as he and Mom got together and decided to have a new house built for the expanding family of five. They bought a lot (think it was $1,000) on the edge of north Duncan. I mean the EDGE, as across the street from our house at 1401 Elder Street was a large (about 35 acres) field occupied by about a hundred prairie dog mounds. Man, what a great place to PLAY! There were no livestock on that field as the animals (cows, horses, sheep) would break their legs in the prairie dog mound "minefield." As long as we dodged the snakes, and there were plenty, as they loved "prairie dog burgers." At the north end (away from our house) was a pond connected to a stream that ran through the north and west sides of the field. Great crawdad, frog and tadpole hunting. A large jar full of tadpoles and crawdads were always on display in our bedroom during the spring and summer. If the tadpoles ventured too low in the bottom of the jar the crawdads caught them. Ouch! Tadpole stew! Keep that pond in mind for a near disaster when snow/ice came to visit with two young boys who were not thinking clearly.

CAMPING OUT

Just before we were able to move into the new house, as it was being built we had to move back "on the other side of the track" for about two months. Our lease on Pine Street was up and we had to "hang out" in a real garage apartment. Indeed, we were truly in an old house's garage that had been committed into a new (?) thing, . . . a garage apartment. It was small and square with a tiny bathroom, a small kitchen and two small bedrooms. Dad stored most of our furniture. We had almost no furniture with one bed (Mom and Dad), stove, refrigerator, table, a couple of chairs and a high chair for Teddy. Bruce and I slept on "perfectly coiffured" blanket pallets (thanks Mom). It was like we were camping out for two months!

Three interesting events occurred while we "camped out." There was a neighborhood grocery store about three houses down from where we "camped." Since Mom was going cabin crazy she was able to give Bruce and me each a nickel each day, then the decisions would take almost all day to decide on which goodie to buy. There was a little boy (about 7) across the street and I used to be amused to watch the icebox operate to keep things cold. It was a real ice box, no electric refrigeration, and the iceman came each day to deliver whatever size block of ice they needed that day. I was amazed at the operation. (Yes, once people really did use <u>real ice boxes</u>!)

Lastly, one day as we were all sitting in the shade under a tree with Teddy sitting in his stroller with a large wooden handle in front of him. He jumped/jerked and smacked his mouth hard on the handle. With blood gushing from Teddy's screaming mouth, guess what happened to one of Teddy's front top teeth. It was hanging down by a strip of flesh, so Dad pulled the hanging tooth. Teddy would be toothless for the next seven years. (We, Mom or Dad later learned from a dentist that the tooth could have been pushed back into his gums. Now we, and you, know.)

STILL BALING

Back to the baling operation which had a pleading operation problem. . . . The baler scooped the hay into the innards of the baler and shaped it into bales (roughly 2 1/2 x 2 1/2 x 4 feet) then wrapped each bale with two strands of heavy twine and tied it. But, when for several reasons sometimes the baler "forgot" to tie one or both twines, so the baler just kept kicking out loose hay. Tilt! When he realized the problem, he had to stop, fix the tying operation and move on. But that was time consuming.

How does Dad fix it? In the rear chute where the bales exit the baler, there is a small seat where someone could just be there to catch such missed-ties. That "inspector" could signal the driver to stop and the miss-tie could then be corrected simply by tying the baler twine. Guess who became the "inspector"? Nine-year-old Tyrus Cobb, Jr. reported for duty! I worked on Saturdays and Sundays when needed and every day from late May through early September each year when I was out of school. (I think I started the summer after second grade.) I loved it, though it was hot, hot and dusty. I wore blue and white striped bid overalls with a straw hat and a large bandana around my neck to control the dust and bits of straw that both flew all over the area where I sat. But, I was happy because I made 50-cents an hour, usually ten hours a day; occasionally Dad gave a bonus of two or three dollars on real tough days, and we had a few.

While I worked in the hay fields I met a lot of nice farmers and their wives who on more than a few times prepared us a great country lunch with whom we ate in their farm homes. Some great eating! I can still remember the lady who served us with chicken and dumplings, . . . humm good! Most of the time though, we had prepared lunches at home; grabbed ourselves a couple of pops (I remember RCs and root beers; do not think Pepsi had made it to Oklahoma at that time) on the way to the fields.

I got pretty good at my job. It was not hard to learn, but working conditions made it tough. I remember several times we baled a snake or two into bales when they got caught in the hay wind-rows. Sometimes Dad let me drive the tractor and he went back to being "inspector" on the rear seat. Man, cool at 9 years old! Once he told me I could drive the tractor (w/o the baler) to the edge of town (about 8 miles) and not to go close, as I was illegal at nine! I had taught myself to get the most speed out of the tractor by shifting the gears and applying overdrive. Man, I was flying on those dirt roads. I was sitting on the edge of town waiting for Dad when he caught up. He wanted to know how I got there so fast. Told him, I just charmed that ole Ford tractor!

I worked with Dad for two summers (1948-49). I made good money for a 9 year old. I made at least $5 each day and sometimes more when we had a big task, like baling 12-13 hours on a day. My first big buy was a brand new, red Rocket bicycle at a big price, $40!

THE STRAINS

I cannot forget a couple who really helped my family during a time when we really needed help. (Wonderful folks.) It was Mel and Red Strain who had become friends of Mom and Dad and those darling Cobb boys. They had a small bakery in Duncan baking bread, cookies, cakes and pies. They had a small staff that began delivering those goodies and bread to local grocery stores. The Strains took a chance, borrowed some money (I am sure), and built a large modern bakery with an oversized back room with several large ovens. Soon they expanded their territory and did well and continued to sell retail at the bakery. I remember being taken to the new bakery many times and mostly just looked at the goodies. I am sure that Bruce was with me when I went there.

Why the help by the Strains? As I recall for some reason, the Strains could not have children, so they took a liking to the young Cobbs, now there three, as Teddy Ney (after Uncle Ted and Grandpa Ney Bagby) born in 1947. We had recently moved into the new house on Elder Street (I think it was 1401 Elder Street of Duncan). Dad had "squared" with Uncle Ted (probably more like his business insurance company of the Duncan Ford Dealership). Dad had surgery on his back in some hospital in Norman or Oklahoma City or somewhere. He was gone over a week and came home with a large cast around his mid-waist up to his breasts. Obviously, he was not very mobile but managed. I remember him taking his personal picture by darkening the breakfast room, opened the shutter of our little box camera and turned the lights on for about five seconds to expose the film. It works. Clever that daddy of ours!

Obviously, Dad was out of work for about two months. It was in the winter so baling was not going and he could not take other work in his condition. There was no money coming in for the Cobbs. (Back then there were no such things as Welfare Checks, . . . there was nothing.) Mom was always a great seamstress, so she took in any sewing jobs she could find and worked at home. Folks, believe we were pretty poor, but the Strains came through.

Almost every night for three months one or both of the Strains came to our house after closing the bakery about eight PM with bread and goodies. Guess we were not eating a great balanced diet, but we were eating! (When we left Duncan in 1950 the bakery was going well, but I do not know what ever happened to those kind people, the Strains. God bless them.)

Dad had two scars on his back one a foot long the other about ten inches. I know Dad was in pain as surgery in the 1940's was not as precise as it is today. I am sure that a man of Dad's condition today would have been better cared for and better surgically corrected than back then. Today his scars would likely be half the size. As baling season approached, Dad toughed it out and got the machinery ready in 1949. Back to the Cobb hay balers of 1950 later.

DUNCAN'S ELDER STREET

About time that I introduce the new house on Elder Street that Mom and Dad had built on a corner lot on the <u>absolute</u> edge north of town. US Highway 81 was one block west of our lot and it went straight north 40 miles to Chickasha. Picture yourself now with us, standing on the lot looking north. A paved town road goes east to west then takes a left turn onto another paved road on the west edge of our lot. Remember we are on a corner lot. (Incidentally, when Dad purchased our lot, the Brumetts also built a home on the same block but on the caddied-corner of the block. We were together again! Yeah, Jay and Marla!!) This is important as I will speak of many cool things that occurred with the Cobbs as they venture their life in that house.

Right across the road (Elder Street) about four or five feet from the road was a deep ditch that paralleled the road and then continued another block to the highway. The ditch was really a drainage ditch, but it was big. It was at least ten feet deep and was shallower on to the west and even deeper if you moved east of our block. When we had a heavy rain, the ditch would be full and roaring up as water gushed draining the area east of us. The ditch was about twelve feet across in front of us, so it contained a lot of water when we had a heavy rain. This normally "sleepy" little stream bed, given a heavy rain, became a vengeful torrent. The ditch's water roared when we had heavy rains and gained the ditch's top, but fortunately it never left the banks. Little boys, be aware of the "menace" across the street from your house.

The field across from us lay to the north. It was roughly the size of a city block (a square in sides of 400 yards each). The topography of the land sloped to the north and to the west. At the north end of the field were two man-made ponds formed by damming up a stream the flowed to the west then south. Two little boys will later head toward those ponds one very cold winter.

Our new house on Elder Street was where we lived and played for my third through first semester of fifth grades. With a major highway just down a slope for a block, a huge "prairie dog town" across the street, a local druggist owner two houses east with three daughters, and do not forget Marla and Jay Brummett who used to live next to us on Pine Street, was set for fun? With that mix of friends and the "lay of the land" it was easy to be in trouble. Hey, we were just kids playing!

Our lot was not landscaped at all! Just dirt and more dirt and weeds and grass stems with three or four stickers ready to pounce on us and goats-head ground level stickers that felt like a blow gun dart had jammed into you bare foot. We used to break off the grass stem with stickers and throw them at each other. They stuck real well to sweaty cotton T-shirts. "Mommy, Bruce is hurting me!"

As one would know, Dad was at it with the new house. He put up a fence with large rolls of wired-together white pickets. Then he dug and built a (tornado) storm cellar. (Everybody in Oklahoma feared tornados and had the urge to go to ground.) It was connected to the back door of the house so that the top of the concrete cellar was about six inches down from the house floor level. He had sunk large bolts into the rim of the cellar roof so he could later build an additional room or screened porch. Clever guy, our dad!

I was now 9-10 and playing little league baseball. But Dad had other things for me to do. When through playing I had to work. The frame of the cellar was made with 1" x 6" and 2" x 4" boards into which concrete was poured. Once set and dried, all the boards had to be pulled off and "cleaned" as well as they could so that the boards could be sold or used to build another item. Guess where I came in? I pulled all the nails out of the boards and scraped the dried cement from the boards.

I remember that Dad always watched the clouds whenever a tornado was eminent and the clouds began to "boil." Even I could see the clouds lower themselves closer to the earth. They were swirling and their colors got really dark and ugly. Winds blew harder and harder. It was enough to scare even adult folks. Dad hand built wooden "bunk beds" in the cellar that would accommodate a half a dozen in beds and another half of dozen of folks standing or sitting on the floor. We spent many a night sleeping in the cellar. What an adventure! And in all those years, we NEVER actually saw a tornado funnel!

We did, however, almost get run over by a runaway horse. Some friend of the Brummetts had ridden their "leisure horse" to visit. The horse was tied to a carpenter's saw-horse when all of the sudden, someone or thing spooked the horse and he jumped a couple of feet. When he did that he pulled the saw horse with him and that really spooked him. That scared him and off he went. By the time he got to our yard the horse was going full speed and dragging the saw-horse behind him. In no time he was nearing U. S. Highway 81. His metal horse shoes caused him to skid, fall, and slide across the highway. I guess the horse was further scared by that fall, as it actually caused him to calm down.

When we could play outside, we used to have "battles." We made scrap lumber swords and pulled tall weeds/bushes and assembled them into forts. Marla was always the queen and I was protecting her against the bad knights, Sir Jay and Sir Bruce.

SATURDAY MOVIES

We were at the young age when we almost always went to Saturday movies. We usually spend all afternoon in the movie house and watched a double feature western and two serials (that would be sure to get us back for the next Saturday). It was not tough to get us back! We each got 20 cents. After each spending 10 cents to get in, we pooled our money to get the greatest value: each got a 5 cent candy bar and then split a 5 cent coke and a 5 cent bag of popcorn.

Main feature entertainment was: Roy Rogers, Gene Autry, Lash LaRue, Johnnie Mac Brown, "Wild Bill" Elliott, Rocky Laine, Tim Holt, Cisco Kid and Poncho, Tex Ritter, Hopalong Cassidy and Rex Allan. For serial entertainment was: Rocket Man, Tarzan, Clyde Beatty (of the jungle), Superman, and Flash Gordon.

In addition to cowboys, there was movie Tarzan played by Johnny Weissmuller (an Olympic champion swimmer), his chimpanzee Cheetah and at times Jane and Boy. In Duncan on the screen, he was in struggles with a giant octopus and later with the Leopard men. Other fun movies, all in black and white were: "Ma and Pa Kettle," "Frances the Talking Mule," "Blondie and Dagwood." We remembered a movie early with Jimmy Stewart and June Allyson, in a true story about a baseball player who had his leg amputated after a hunting trip accident, named "The Monty Stratton Story." Also, saw a movie "short" topic about West Point when I was about nine in Duncan.

Cartoons were many and all well-received by the kiddie "peanut gallery!" Among our favorites were: Mickey and friends; Woody Woodpecker; Heckle and Jeckle, the zany crows; Mighty Mouse; Poppey; and Droopy the dog.

I "saw" Gene Autry at the new Will Rogers elementary school in Duncan. Well, I did not actually see him, but we kids in the fourth grade were introduced to music via a record player. The teacher had the latest Christmas record coming out of Hollywood, CA by one of our movie heroes, Gene Autry, the singing cowboy. We would have thought he would be singing a cowboy song, but no, it was a Christmas song "Rudolph the Red-Nosed Reindeer." That was in Christmas time 1949 and that song took off on all the radios in America, including Duncan, Oklahoma. (And it has not stopped, as I heard it several times this Christmas time in 2020!) Its popularity has not waned.

Another very popular Christmas song that came out about the same time was "I Saw Mommy Kissing Santa Claus Underneath the Mistletoe." by a young boy (probably about 12 years old) named Jimmy Boyd. That song is still heard occasionally but not as often as old Gene. (Gene made a pile of money making movies and today his estate makes another pile with "Rudolph". He became {years ago} the principal owner of the California Angels baseball team and a lot of Hollywood real estate.)

(Today {2021} my favorite Christmas song is "Holly, Jolly Christmas" by Burl Ives another oldster, but "Rudolph" still brings a smile to my face every time I hear Gene sing his story.)

While speaking of Christmas things, we all loved the Christmas tree lights that Mom and Dad must have purchased early in their marriage. There were about 30 lights in the string. Most of the lights were basic colored (red, blue and green) lights but there were about 10 bulbs that were themed lights, e.g., a snowy house, a snowman and I remember two big bells, one red and one blue. The lights were likely purchased in the early 1940's, so they were in series (one light burned out, none would light up). Bruce and I always sat and marveled at the lights.

Around 1949 Mom bought some new technology Christmas tree lights. They were "bubble" lights that one could clip up on the tree. The heat of the light heated up some type of fluid in a clear vial that looked light colored water and after about a minute it bubbled. Another marvel for Bruce, Teddy and me to set and watch, watch and watch!

Mom made us both to take a bath before we went to the Saturday matinee movies. We knew from last week's serial feature that "Superman was in trouble" and we would be there to see how he "escaped." To get ready Bruce tied a towel around his neck and decided to "fly." He ran speedily through the hall into the living room and at his full speed he jumped into a large chair and his momentum had the chair "fly" into the large window that broke out a pane of the main picture window. The next day there was a little article in the Duncan paper about Bruce showing Superman how to get out of a tight situation. Believe or not, that same Saturday serial, plot saw Superman also fly through a glass window to "escape!"

In the springtime, we always had tadpoles and crawdads in jars in our room. We also had terrapins of various sizes in a box and one rather unique creature only found in the southwest. Horny toads! We worked as a team to catch them as they were fast. Occasionally, we would get ourselves into a "nest" of babies. They were "cute," but prehistoric looking. The little ones had flat round bodies about two inches across, while the adults were about four inches across. I had heard of larger ones but never saw one.

On a winter day it can get pretty cold, even in Oklahoma. For sure open water will freeze. Bruce and I wrapped ourselves up and headed outside to play. Yes, it was cold! For some reason we decided to go to the pond across the street from us and at the far north end of prairie dog town. When we were about halfway there Mom realized that we were on our way to the pond. She was terrified thinking that we might fall through the ice. She left Teddy by himself and crawled on her hands and knees across the icy 2" x 12" board across the ditch and raced to catch us just as we reached the pond. She was crying uncontrollably and told us we had scared her to death and that Dad was going to deal with us when he came home from work.

We had to wait about six hours until Dad got home. Waiting those six hours, in our little minds we realized what we had done that would cause a parent grief. Mom told Dad what we had done. I guess Dad was so happy that we had not been hurt (thanks to Mom) that he scowled us and that was it. For us, however, six hours of waiting for Dad to come home was punishment enough.

SKIPPER JOINS THE FAMILY

One day as I walked home from third grade at Emerson school a young, solid black, part cocker spaniel and part terrier dog followed me home. He was friendly and every loved him. But Mom said we had to see if we could find the dog's owner. Of course, we hoped Mom could not find the owner. She did and told them she would bring him back. Guess she told the owner how her boys loved the dog. She said we could have the dog and even gave Mom two cans of dog food!

We named our new dog "Skipper" because he actually had a "skip" in his left hind leg as he walked along. (We had him for nine years as he moved around from Duncan to Chickasha and Claremore. In Claremore, he was out chasing "women" when he tangled with a tougher dog that bit a huge bite out of his throat. Poor guy. He had to be put down.)

One night a kitten, from one of the dentist's girls three houses away east of us, crawled into our back yard. I was out playing and I grabbed the kitten and was walking it over to one of the girls. All of a sudden Skipper "charged" barking. The kitten panicked and clawed several bloody scratches the length of my back through my sweaty t-shirt. Mom to the rescue! Kitten over the fence and blood wiped.

Mom and Dad also loved baseball and to "pay" me for all the

good work (and it was good; de-nailing and cleaning the boards used in building our storm cellar) they told me they were going to take me to the local team game. Hey, concrete bleachers, huge lights, and a concession stand! Think they bought me a coke and popcorn. About half way through the game they asked me if they thought I could go to the stand and get two cups of coffee. Sure! Mistake. I paid for the cups of hot coffee . . . 5 cents each. As I starting carrying the cups, one in each hand, the jiggling of (steaming hot) coffee caused it to trickle out on to my hands. It has a long way to their seats and my hands started to burn, but I was not going to drop them and get them to my folks. Tears came to my eyes but I walked on. By the time I got to them all the folks around were feeling and cheering for me. But I got to them with hot coffee. What a stud! Maybe I grew up a little that night.

Also that night, folks were shooting off a lot of big fireworks as it was Fourth of July (some folks like to call it Independence Day). We liked the fireworks at the ball game, but when we got home (about ¾ of a mile from the ball park), oh my gosh, poor Skipper almost had a doggie heart attack. The fireworks had scared Skipper out of his wits and he clawed and chewed the back door screen and part of the back asbestos shingles on the side of the house. We felt so sorry for what he had gone through that evening; he lived. (BTW, we thought we had a new, modern type of shingles and we were told that the asbestos was also fire-proof. Of course, they truly did not know then that asbestos was also cancer-causing.)

One fulfilling of our sweet teeth was Mom's fudge. Never tasted any better before or after. She just "nursed" the recipe on the Hershey's cocoa container. It had to be just right after it came to a near boil; boil was not good, so she stirred and stirred. She looked to see if a drop of the concoction would form a ball in cold water; then it is ready to be poured out on a platter and let cool. Then it was ready for Bruce and I to do our job – licking the pan and spoon! (I have looked through many a Hershey's cocoa container for that recipe, but alas it must be history.)

Mom very occasionally (because it did not snow enough) made "snow ice cream." Had to first snow once before making the ice cream; you see, Mom said it had to snow first to clear the air, then the second snow was ready for making. She used sugar, vanilla and a little milk and "viola, let's eat!"

TY COBB ENTERS ORGANIZED BASEBALL

And then I began playing organized baseball. Dad bought me a five fingered glove, and he played a lot of "catch" with me. Our team played a team in Velma, OK (a small oil town about 15 miles from Duncan) and I got my first try at pitcher. I liked it, but I did not know how well I did. One thing I did well that I remembered. The hitter I pitched to fouled the ball toward the first base line toward the catcher's right. I went after it and made a diving catch for an out! I was proud until the coach told me to let the catcher take those balls. Learning the game, but I made a good catch!

With a few games under our belts, we were getting ready to enter a big (about a dozen teams) tournament in Duncan on the four baseball field complex. The coach (also owner of sports store) issued each a uniform (gray flannel) and red cotton stirrup hose. Mom washed the uniform and stirrup hose so I would look clean at the games. I do not remember how I played that day, but I do remember how I looked in my pink uniform (thanks to the new red stirrups washing with the uniforms) and I was the talk of Duncan's youth baseball players and parents alike!

Halloween time was always a fun time. Naturally, we put on costumes, at least a mask, and knocked on as many houses' doors as we could seeking treats. Then we would have treats for a good week's time. Another event was Halloween Carnivals at school for fun and raising funds to buy things that improved the school. Every room had a gimmick with moms and teachers working each room classes' fun thing: Wishing Well; dart toss; and my favorite, the Cake Walk. Just seeing everyone in their costumes was an added treat.

Our new house had five rooms: living room, kitchen, breakfast room, two bedrooms, plus a small bath room. We three boys each had a door to the long (room width length) closet. The walls of the room were wall-papered with cowboys and were really loved by the three little buckaroos. When we could not play outside, we always played "cowboys and Indians" in the house. Bruce and I took our pillows and wrapped a belt around the "horses'" neck and our saddles were ready to "mount our steed" which served as horses (foot board of our double bed). We served as the bad guy running from the sheriff. Eventually the "good guy would catch up with the bad guy and would jump from the rear horse to the lead horse and roll the bad guy off into the dust for a capture." Now if you don't understand that game, just use a little imaginary, buckaroo!

I think that Mom had taken dance lessons as a youth and Granny Bagby liked to do a little gig hoofing herself. Anyway, Mom and the mother of a little girl a couple of blocks down Elder Street (Duncan) teamed us to take square dancing every Sunday afternoon for about 10 weeks. After us first dancing with just "plain" clothes, Mom got to work with her sewing machine and came up with a green plaid cotton cloth and made me a long-sleeved shirt (wore jeans with it) and the girl a long full dress of the same cloth. To this date, when I see pictures of the two of us in the dancing outfits I marvel at the works of art that Mom created for us to wear, especially Barbara Elwell's dress. I really took to the square dancing, but never did it again. However, Barbara was a cutie and I was still handsome. Well, I thought so!

Barbara's family moved away, but I saw her briefly when I played in that Velma, OK baseball game when I played there and caught that foul ball.

Besides playing inside and outside, we loved to listen to the afternoon kids' radio shows. There were Tom Mix and his horse, Tony; Sky King and his nephew (do not remember his name) and niece, Penny; Straight Arrow and his golden Palomino, Fury; the Lone Ranger and his horse, Silver, and his companion, Tonto, and his horse, Scout; Sergeant Preston of the Northwest Mounted Police and his great dog, King; and several others I cannot remember. I also remember several more mature shows we listened with our folks: The Shadow; Amos and Andy; Fibber McGee and Molly; and the Jack Benny Show sponsored by Lucky Strikes. Before television, the radio always had a huge audience of which I was one, but TV was on the way to American audiences.

Besides radio shows for us kiddies were, of course, several games in which we availed ourselves. The fare were: Jigsaw puzzles, Chinese Checkers with a marble board, regular Checkers, Parcheesi, card games like Old Maids and Authors, Monopoly, and Pick-up-Sticks. One Christmas I got an Elector Set that I built a variety of model things like towers, bridges, windmills and others with an electric motor that was part of the set. And, of course, electric trains were a favorite; one was a silver passenger train that I got when I was three years old and played with it for a decade and a half!

Mom's Creations

Duncan built a new elementary school near us and we transferred from Emerson School to the new Will Rogers Elementary school. I was in the fourth grade and Bruce entered school in the first grade. Assignment to that new school was my first introduction to the name, Will Rogers. You will "see" him again as I write forward.

As I was excited about our new school, I kept standing up to get a peek at the goings-on outside as a bit of equipment was driving around and a couple of men were working. The principal, Mr. Hudson, walked in and the teacher said she could not get Master Cobb to stay in his desk. Mr. Hudson said, "let's go outside, Master Cobb." I thought he was going to hit me out there. He told me to stand there and watch and until I had seen enough. Two minutes and I was ready to go in. Psychology 101! It worked perfectly. I stayed in my seat for a long while.

Dad was finding some houses to rent in Chickasha so the family could join him at the new job. Still, we had to find a buyer for our home in Duncan and his baling equipment.

Then Bruce came home from school with black and blue bruises on his behind as he had been paddled for misbehavior. Mom was furious, then so was Dad when he got home. It was okay to spank but not so hard that it left the marks on Bruce's behind. Mom took him out of school. We were going to move in a few weeks, so Bruce stayed home and entered the second grade in West School near the home we rented in Chickasha. Bruce did fine passing the second grade. (Years later, Bruce admitted that he probably deserved the paddling, but he had no idea what he did.)

Me (age 4) and my "sidekick"
Bruce (1)

We grew into "kid lawmen"

Bad guys better
watch out!

VACATIONING WITH MISSOURI BAGBYS

At this point I want to take time to tell you about our vacations primarily to the grand folks Cobb and Bagby. The Cobbs resided as long as I knew them in the same place. My dad and his kin lived in the same house in Elk City, Oklahoma for their entire lives. That is where we visited or vacationed with the grand folks Horace Dixon Cobb and his wife, Pearl.

The Bagby grand folks resided in two places for all the time when we visited. The first was in a country grocery (etc.) store. They worked that store for several years then when they sold it and with money they had saved they bought, about 160 acres of rich farm land within 5 straight miles of the Mississippi River. The land was extremely fertile, as thousands of years earlier the river had flooded many times and deposited fertile silt. Grandpa Bagby raised cotton and soybeans, as well as, a small herd of Hereford cattle.

But the first memory of my Bagbys was when they ran the country store on the White River. The store was right on a country dirt road and next to the store was the wooden bridge that crossed the river. The bridge was about thirty feet above the river, and it sported a single lane that had wooden "planks" to guide a vehicle moving over the bridge which had no side railings. Listen here . . . you better pay attention! Bruce and I, as well as several other children (from knows where) swam in the river in the shade of the bridge. It had a slow current, was about two feet deep, and had a sandy bottom. When rains came, the river rose and its current multiplied -- no more swimming in the river!

Bruce and I fished with Dad in the river and I do not remember catching anything. One day while there, Dad saw a snake about four feet (okay, three feet) long swimming in the river just below the country store and called for Grandpa's shotgun. Snake be gone! Nice shot, Dad!

I only remember vacationing there once, but my Uncle Bill Bagby's family later owned a section (640 acres) of good land for cotton and soybeans. I think Uncle Bill inherited the land from an uncle from Grandma Bagby's family of the Rhineharts. Grandpa and Granny's country store was on the edge of Uncle Billy's section because it was bordered by the river. That was later, but initially Uncle Bill's family lived in the really small town of Lilbourn, Missouri. Lilbourn was in the very lower of the southeast corner of the state of Missouri. Towns of New Madrid, Kennett, Marston, Portageville, Hayti, Risco, Maldon and distant Sikeston ring a bell in this old memory of mine. Just thought you would want to know.

The Harry and Nina Bagbys invested their savings and purchased their quarter section of land and became farmers; cotton, soy beans and Hereford beef cattle. They built a small home of two bedrooms, kitchen, dining room, living room and bathroom. The house was about seventy yards from an extremely busy US 61 (today Interstate 55) with heavy truck traffic. Boy, did we ever love being there! (More on that later.) The house was about three miles from Lilbourn where Uncle Bill's family lived, as well as, some Rinehart relatives.

Grandpa Bagby had a sharecropper family live in a house on his land who earned a living by helping him plant and bring in the crops, cotton and soybeans. The sharecroppers were white, but I learned that there were a lot of Black folks who made a living by sharecroppers. Early on, I learned the sharecropper's house had an outhouse and got their water with a hand pump well. Well, some would consider us "poor" but we learned that we really had a "lot." We had known that some folks had more than we, now we were learning that some also had much less than we did.

The "place" was Grandpa's place to share with Grandma, of course. Besides the house, the place had a wide rock gravel driveway, a chicken coop with three sections, a three bay garage, no doors, with dirt floor which had an anvil, lots of hand tools like hoes for chopping cotton (you do not actually "chop cotton," you chop weeds out from around cotton plants). Besides the chicken yard (about an acre), land was committed to farming income, about twenty acres for cattle and the rest for cotton and soybeans.

We usually went to Missouri in the summer, as we were out of school. Once when I was in the third grade, I was in an Easter time kiddie play. I was Peter Cotton Tail, of "hopping down the bunny trail" fame, and sang a little rabbit ditty. Mom, of course, was the creator of my costume that was much like a full length pajama suit only it also had a rabbit head and a pair of long ears; all in pink, of course. Also had a big red patch on my behind, you see I (the bunny) had been raiding the vegetable patch. Guess we were going to Missouri to show everybody the new boy baby, Teddy Ney Cobb, aged four months. Uncle Bill Bagby (Mom's brother) drove us to Missouri for a week when we were supposed to be in school. . . . hey, Grandma needs to see baby Teddy!

TRAVELLING BY CAR

Strange . . ., but I do not remember what kind of car we had (except the T-Model Ford that Dad had "converted" into a "pick-up"), but we got there. Do not remember the car, but boy do I remember some of the things we did and saw! The trip to get to Missouri started in middle Oklahoma, then diagonally south to north through the whole state of

Arkansas then into southeast Missouri. Sometimes we went through Little Rock; I remember cable trolleys there. (The first family car I remember was a 1952 four-door light green Chevrolet, but that was in the mid-fifties.)

The roads we traversed are all paved today, but back then you never knew what you would run into. Some roads of the region (OK, AR and MO) had two-way two lanes paved roads, others had two way roads with only one lane paved, the other gravel, and lastly, some were just gravel roads.

Getting across rivers was an experience. Not a few of the bridges we encountered were likely built in the 1910 to 1920 time frame for lighter vehicles like horse-drawn wagons and Model T Fords. They did not make you feel comfortable to try your luck in conquering those scary bridges and the angry looking river under it! The roadway platform of many bridges were steel frames with wooden planks laid and fastened down, then beckoned folks to try their luck. After a few years of traffic, it was not unusual to see holes or even planks missing affording us a straight down view into the river. Yes, it was scary, especially at flood time, as rivers were raging!

Having a bridge was a luxury in some areas in rural Arkansas. We had to cross some rivers, but there were no bridges. We would leave the road, whatever conditions of the road, and transfer to a single lane with 2 x 12 planks laid in the mud or dirt. Motorists drove downhill to the river, then boarded a motorized ferry to cross the river. It could ferry folks across the river even when flood stage occurs; if a flood was too vicious, one would see ferry operations cease. These 2 x 12 plank "roads" could be picked up when the rivers began to overflow its banks and rise from the river onto the river's flood plain. This rise could be a few inches or a colossal flood.

Though I do not remember the kind of car we had, they were all four-doors and were roomy inside, as that was the way most cars were configured in the late forties. Bruce and I were "kings" of the back seat.

I always (still do to an extent) tending to get car sick, sometimes to the point of vomiting. Riding in the back seat made the sickness develop easier and quicker. But I was stuck there so did the best usually with windows open, remember most cars did not have air conditioners and we certainly did not. Best help for car sickness was to sleep, and I made a pallet in the back seat floor. Of course, we all had our pillows.

On long (several hundred miles) trips Mom always made our trek vittles, fried chicken, buttered-bread and a thermos of folks' coffee and one for water. (If you miss-treated those thermos they would break inside and they had to be thrown away.) This was really necessary, as there were no McDonalds or KFCs all over the place like today. There might be a "greasy spoon" café in a town, but you had to be careful what you might be eating. Dad would stop in some places and buy a bag with six hamburgers for a dollar! Other times he would purchase a pound of baloney, cheese (both cut by hand machine) and a loaf of bread.

Once in a while we were happy to run into regional "gasoline wars." Filling stations were lowered and lowered their price for gasoline to try to get customers to use their brands, e.g., Skelly, Phillips and Sinclair. Say the normal price was 30 cents a gallon, we would see some stations with the price as low as 15 cents a gallon!

Motels were almost non-existence in the small towns in Oklahoma, Arkansas and Missouri so we "camped out," in the car! I remember once when Dad drove well into the night during a light snow storm, and the headlights really lit up the snowflakes which scared us. At least me! The lights reflected from the snowflakes which made it difficult to see in the night. By the way, there were almost no lights on the road or in the surrounding fields. We usually left home for vacations in the late morning time, thus we would eventually end up to the night and Dad drove hard until he was too tired to continue. With few places to rent for a night's sleep and they were never in our money range anyway, so Dad would find the safest place to park that he could find. Windows were cracked a bit, doors locked and parked usually in front a police station! We never had a problem, at least that I know of! Thank you, Lord.

[Today a motorist can buy a modern car. Keep it oiled, rotate the tires and feed it gasoline and you can run it for 100,000 miles without a problem.] In the 1940s there was always something going wrong, especially during a 600 mile trip. But, we could always depend on Dad to fix it. We had over heating when the engine cooling system had trouble keeping water cool enough to regulate the engine temperature. Unless we had a bad leak, Dad just turned on the compartment heater which in turn served as an "alternate water cooler" for the engine water. It worked! Got a flat? Done. Got a broken fan belt? That is one thing that Dad always carried--an extra fan belt. We never broke down for more than half an hour. Thanks, Dad. Moving on to Missouri! (Elk City was only about a three hours trip –no problem there.)

FUN AT GRANNY BAGBYS

We vacationed at the grand folk Bagbys several times from the later 1940s into the 1950s. Of course, our grand folks were just outside of Lilbourn where Uncle Bill Bagby's family lived. Bruce and I always took a baseball and our gloves to visit so we could play together while there. Grandpa Bagby was a rabid St. Louis Cardinal fan and listened to almost all their games on the radio. (Remember there was no television then.) Our other play game there was to stand in the front yard, about 50 feet from highway US 61 as the traffic zoomed by. The highway was alive with semi-trailer/tractors (about 8-10 a minute). The tractor, carrying the driver and pulling the trailer, usually had a real loud horn that slaved air from the brake system and ran it through the horn. So, cool! Most of the drivers would sound a couple of "toot, toots" to say "hey" if you pumps your fist up and down a few times simulating that you were pulling an air horn lanyard. Man, what great fun to be recognized!

Bruce and I thought the Bagbys were cool folks, probably because they liked to "entertain" us. I remembered watching grandpa rolling his Bull Durham cigarettes, and the top (from eye brow upward) of his head was very white as he worked all day in the sun with his cowboy hat on. He never raised his voice and loved to just look at us at whatever we were doing. He had been a hard- working man for most of his life. Once he had operated a "steam shovel" (today run by motor engines and much bigger) and was one such operator in the building of the Oakland Bay Bridge in California. (By the way, Mom, when a youngster while living there, skipped a grade in school due to her intelligence. Guess we all took after her!)

Granny Bagby was in charge of things in and outside the yard including the big chicken shed. It had one section in which the hens nested to lay eggs. Another shed had a lock system that kept the chickens and other small animals out of the corn and was used to store dry corn on the cob. However, there were several other critters, e.g., field mice, that managed to get into that section and feast on the dry corn. Bruce and I found that snakes also managed to get into that corn storage section. Hey, those snakes did not eat corn? That's right. But they feasted on the corn-fed mice that were "stealing" Granny's corn. We often retrieved corn to feed the chickens, but we always kept a close eye out for Mr. Snake. Mr. Mouse always had our attention because there were so many of them.

Earlier when I got my BB gun for Christmas (Bruce got one too when I did) I thought I was a big hunter, so sparrows became my game as Dad had told me sparrows were dirty birds. Actually, they were no dirtier than any other bird. But I sought them as big game. When I "bagged" one, I got Mom's finger nail polish and put little red circles on the barrel of the gun. I was up to seven when I felt sorry for the poor little critters and I quit.

Behind the three-bay, dirt floor garage was the family trash bin, a five by three feet by three feet tall metal bin that was normally used to contain water to water down the large animals. Actually, it was not a garbage bin, because no garbage was there to throw out because the garbage was feasted upon by the chickens and small animals. Who would think Bruce and I would have fun with a trash bin? Well, we did! We placed a board across the bin lengthways, set up jars and bottles on the board, then loaded up our BB guns. (We were "much older" now and had received BB guns from Santa last Christmas.) We could shoot to our hearts content and the broken glass and cans fell harmlessly into the bin.

Granny Bagby was a great cook, but she demanded good manners at the dinner table. She even taught us how to hold a fork and knife politely while eating—if right handed, place the fork level with the plate and the tings facing down with the left hand and the knife in the right hand. Hold (the meat) with the fork and cut it with the right. Bruce, being left-handed, did the opposite.

I guess when the builder of the Bagbys' home they did not dig the well very deep, as the water was tainted by sulfur making the water smell like rotten eggs. And, the pump was very, very slow in drawing water. To draw a bath of about four inches deep took about half an hour. The water also tasted bad. Granny had a case of six ounce glass-bottled Cokes in the kitchen and kept a few in the frig, but she allowed only one each per day. She also made ice tea that helped to kill the water's taste. I reckon we survived the water taste, but it is a vivid memory of us all. That covers our liquid input at Granny's house.

Now for food! Granny was a great country food cook. Her best was frying one of her chickens right out of the chicken yard. None fresher than that! So we ate well, but clean what was on your plate; you asked for it; eat it! But what was Granny's piece de resonant? Her upside-down pineapple cake. Her banana cake was not bad either. She always cooked one when we came and that was one of the things we dreamed about as we rode to Missouri.

COUSINS HAVE HORSES

When in Missouri we stayed with the grand folks, but we went into Lilbourn often to socialize with Uncle Billy and Aunt Eva's family. Between Uncle Billy's house and a larger house, pretty old and big, and where we met Aunt John; the large pasture also belonged to Uncle Billy. Yes, she was called "John." She was loud and I understand she drank a "bit." An older lady also lived with Aunt John, who she might have been my great grandma by the name of Bullock. Anyway, a large barbed wired pasture that was about a block in size and between Aunt John's and Uncle Bill's homes was where Uncle Billy kept his horses and ponies for his daughters, Gail and Billie Anne. Gail was a year older than I and Billie Ann was same age as Bruce. Both girls were small, as were Uncle Billy and Aunt Eva, but, boy, they could really ride their horses. (Both would later ride professionally in many rodeo barrel races. Gail succumbed to cancer in the 1990's and, as far as, I know, Billie Anne still rides in California.)

The girls "trained" us to ride horses, and drink Pepsi! Bruce was a good rider. I rode, but I was pretty much a failure. One of the first times I rode in Lilbourn I remember being in the saddle in Aunt John's yard where someone was trying to remove a large tree's roots and a ditch had been dug all around the stump. It was about five feet deep. The pony I was riding decided he was tired of me, and knew how to un-ass me. When he was saddled, he pushed out his innards to make his waist larger than usual. At his decision, he sucked in his girth, the saddle girth belt was now too large to hold on to the horse and the saddle slide off on to his belly which threw me into the ditch. On my first ever pony ride I thought I had been killed, as I had my breath knocked out which I had never experienced before. Maybe that is why I never really was fond of horse, but I rode for pride. A sissy cowboy!

There had been a few catchy popular songs played often on the radio at that time and for some reason I fancied a few and "sang" them. My folks had me sing them for relatives. Probably embarrassed, but I sang on cue for the crowd. The song that sticks in my choral repertoire was "Sioux City Sue," a country song that was big in America's country folks. If I had ever learned guitar back then, maybe I would had competed with Elvis. Nah!

However, every year we went to the Billy Bagby's house, saddled ponies and rode around Billy's side of Lilbourn with Gail and Billie Ann imagining we were cowboys on a cattle ride. Yee haw! I really looked like a cowboy with my blue and white stripped bib overalls, red straw cowboy hat and sun glasses. City boy goes country!

Me (1945) on back porch of Pine St. house with my first fish from Lake Duncan

Dad and I pond fishing w/cane poles in Duncan. (Age 10.) Bruce & Teddy sitting.

Me at Uncle Bill's yard decked out as a "drug store" cowboy c. 1948

Me working on my "movie" actions. (back of Elder St., Duncan) c. 1950

I vaguely remember something about Uncle Bill having a roller skating building about a block from his house. There was a juke box to play records (78 rpm) for the customers to skate with the music. People may have paid to skate, but Uncle Bill surely made money on songs for a nickel and soda pop and candy for a dime. I remember us getting a free soda.

Even though Uncle Billy's house was "in town" they had to use an outhouse. Classy, because they had a "two-holer"! Like most outhouses, theirs was quite "airy" with flies and hornets flying all over the place, and hornets' nests too! I was always afraid that I was going to get stung. We survived.

Teddy was seven younger than me, so during our trips to Missouri Bruce and I did not play much with him though he was there. Teddy had a "seeing" problem. He could see well but he could not look straight at people. He had to turn his head about 15 degrees to the side (his left I think). Our parents were good parents and they worried about how Teddy might worsen as he got older. They searched for an eye surgeon that could help. Believe me back then there were not a lot of doctors that could help. Mom had found a surgeon in Little Rock that thought he could help. I remember on one of our trips to Missouri that we sat outside a small clinic in Little Rock where the doctor practiced. We got there in the evening and waited outside for about an hour before they would take Teddy. It was about nine at night. Teddy did get an operation later that helped correct the turning of his head for seeing people but there was still a small turn for the rest of his life, though he saw well. (Actually, when Teddy got older all the girls thought that was sexy. I wonder if Elvis copied that from Teddy?)

Later Uncle Billy and Aunt Eva and their girls moved into a nice, but small, house that was on the 640 acres they owned. Of course, they had ponies. Billie Ann saddled us up and off Bruce, she and I took off across as the soybean fields. Billie Ann and Bruce started running their horses, and I did not like that. I thought they were making my horse run and maybe they did. I unassed the horse and plowed into the field unhurt. See the horseback cowboy wimp walk home! My horse had fun, he ran with the other two.

Uncle Bill had a valuable piece of land that would yield a good living, the 640 cotton/soy bean acres. But, he got to dreaming and I guess he wanted to be a big rancher. The last I remember us visiting them, his family was in Black Rock, Arkansas on a 3,000 acre "ranch." I was about 15 then. Uncle Bill traded his 640 of great farming land for 3,000 acre of scrub oak, a couple of ponds/lakes, a big barn and a small house and 200 head of sheep! Baaaa! We rode horses. I did for <u>one</u> day and Bruce, as usual, rode every day with Billie Ann while we were there. I laid around the house and read Uncle Bill's "True Detective" magazines.

[We never visited the Arkansas "ranch" again, as we had other things going (do not really remember what, but there were things like baseball and summer football and working at a small neighborhood grocery store). Uncle Bill later had a travelling rodeo featuring the girls. I remember we all went to Joplin, Missouri one evening and visited Uncle Bill's rodeo there. Patsy introduced us to "Rodeo Steak and Champagne" (hamburgers and Pepsi). Aunt Eva passed with cancer and Uncle Bill died a few years later. Gail got married and had a son; she also died of cancer relatively young. I lost track of Billie Ann but last I heard she lived in California still riding horses.]

For a while, let us turn to visiting the grandparents Cobb (H.D. and Pearl) in Elk City, OK.

VACATIONING WITH THE OKLAHOMA GRAND-COBBS

Elk City was where the H.D. Cobb children (one my Dad, Tyrus) spend most of their younger days. Etha was the oldest child and the only girl; so she had a small bedroom off the dining room to herself. They all attended the 1-12 school for Elk City. Went I first went to Elk City, I remembered things such as where there was a neighborhood grocery store. When I visited there "candy heaven" was but a short (about 100 feet) walk if a few pennies was to be had.

My dad used to tell my brothers and I how tough they had to walk to school. (His nose was "growing!") Elk City's 1-12 school was on the next block from their house! Except for the first grade at the Catholic School in Duncan, we never had a walk closer than four blocks. In Claremore, we truly were about a mile from high school where we all attended and we walked that mile many times.

The H. D. Cobb children lived in the same Elk City house for most of their lives. The house was relatively large with a living room, four bedrooms, a large dining room and a large kitchen. The house also had a large enclosed back porch. Just out the back door was a dirt mound cellar. It was for protection, as Oklahoma was "famous" for tornadoes. Grandma Cobb was "famous" for all of her canned foods. I loved her apricot preserves, but she had a real load of canned fruits and vegetables all grown in her large back yard. We usually took about a dozen jars of canned foods home every time we visited.

For some family event, of which I do not know, all the sons and daughter rounded up in Elk City. Motels? Ha-ha, are you kidding? We all boarded in the family house. All bedrooms were taken leaving more than a few "bed less." The sons borrowed three or four mattresses from a friend's store and laid them on the living room floor and we all slept there, about ten of us! Wonder who was the last one asleep around-- midnight!

The Cobbs had an upright piano in the living room and Grandma was a great pianist. She was the local Baptist church pianist. She would play for us at home and sometimes she would really get "rollin" and you would think she was Jerry Lee Lewis! I also remember her playing after Grandpa was gone and she would play songs he and she had loved and she would, with tears streaming down her face, be thinking about him. She loved the man. Everybody did!

Grandma did not like smoking. Her sons could get away with doing it, but she almost forbid the ladies of smoking in her house. My Mom and other ladies were always playing how to get a quick smoke in without getting caught!

BYE-BYE PHILLIPS 66

I remember when the Elk City Cobbs sold the Phillips business and were wondering what they should now do, as they did not want to just sit. On their property they had two "garage" apartments built. The apartments were a down one apartment and an upper. They were small, but just perfect for couples. When occupied, the grand folks had a nice income. I guess grandpa was restless again, so they bought the local General Electric store. Things went along nicely until one day about ten months after they had opened the store, while talking to a friend outside the store, grandpa Cobb walked into the store and fell dead of a heart attack. Strangely, he was 66 years old and had worked years for US Phillips 66. At the time we were living on Texas Street in Chickasha, so we loaded into the car and went to Elk City. I was a little apprehensive, but they took me to the wake and I saw my first dead person, my grandpa Cobb.

The road trip to Elk City was about three hours and to Lilbourn was about eleven hours, so the Cobb boys could get real bored. Real bored! During flood periods watching the raging rivers under <u>our car</u> on scary looking bridges really got our attention and, . . ., yes, scared. "Hey, Bruce, look at those cows." "Ty, look at those horses." "What the heck are those?" "Goats, stupid."

We would see who would say "Punch Bug! I got it first." Volkswagen or beetle or bug was novel back then and to see one got your attention. So, we made it a counting game to pass the passenger travel time away. Another vehicle that thrilled us was by a "convoy," which was a large semi-trailer truck that hauled four new cars. (Guess we liked them because one time Dad worked as a Chevrolet salesman in Chickasha.) Hauling four cars on a big truck was thought to be cool by the little Cobb boys. (Just the other day I saw a "modern convoy" hauling <u>nine</u> new cars. Progress one might say.)

As farms rolling on and on and on in our view, we saw big ones, little ones, neat ones and shabby ones. The lack of rain and poor farming techniques led to America's Great Dust Bowl in the '20s and '30s. The damaged farm land, especially in western Oklahoma, was part of that phenomena, and we saw a panoramic view of it as three little Cobb boys traveled to Elk City. We saw a tortured landscape on display with the erosion effects that had yielded such poor farming like failure to employ contour plowing. I remember in high school studying such and other smart farming methods that corrected poor farming. But folks, that took three or four decades to yield productive farming. [From the fifties to the 2010 days when Bruce and I once again drove through western Oklahoma to Elk City we saw corporate farming well managed and beautiful farm production again.]

Another "neat" sight along the roads of western Oklahoma was on many a field post were coyote carcasses nailed unto. They were hunted with a vengeance because they killed many a young calf. Beef cattle were a huge commodity produced in the state. Do not tread on my land!

West of Oklahoma City the topography becomes really flat and roads are straight, straight, straight. On our trips to Elk City, we approached a county seat town on State Route 152. We drove about 50 miles on the road which brought us straight into Cordell, OK, that had been laid out like a really neat classic town square with a three story Court House for that county. We could see that Court House for about six or seven miles as we approached it. We knew we were less than an hour to grand-folks house. We usually stopped in a filling station there to hit the rest room and get a Dr. Pepper for all. That Dr. Pepper was had by putting nickels in a machine. One nickel yields one cold six ounce, glass bottled Dr. Pepper.

STOP! THIEF!

Dad gave me five nickels and sent me to get the Dr. Peppers. I came back with 7 nickels and 6 Dr. Peppers! The machine obviously malfunctioned and "gave" me with the loot. Dad said, "Get in the car." We headed for Elk City and drank our six ounce Dr. Peppers. Now for our get away on Route 152.

For 27 miles via Route 152 we came to State Road 6 which is a 90 degree right turn onto State 6 and seven miles to Elk City. At that turn was a small filling station which at times had gasoline, but don't count on it. That seven mile stretch was flat with just tan grass growing. I don't even remember a single building all the way to Elk City.

Five years later, . . . Boom Town! Oil was discovered on that seven-mile stretch along State Road 6 and now was covered with pumps pulling oil from the good earth and derricks all over drilling for more. And one more thing that amused me. The "rough necks" implanted pipes into the underground oil pools to bleed methane gas out of the ground, and they simply burned it off 24/7. (Today, that methane is capped and sold as an expensive by-product of the oil industry. I remember when I was a teenager and saw burn off pipes I imagined that there must be some way to use that burn-off gas. Duh!)

MR. OWL

Now for the Tyrus, Sr. Chickasha Cobbs when they were at their cruelest, most shameful, and stupidest when they met upon "Mr. Owl" on the road from Elk City to Chickasha. Not sure but I think I was about ten and we were in the car on our way home from grandpa's home. For some reason, we probably had to stop to pee. Where Dad pulled off the road was in a cut out where the dirt wall was about fifteen high on the sides of the road. Suddenly Dad yelled, "Look, boys!" In a small hole of the dirt wall was a full grown owl. He was beautiful! And, he was fearsome looking to us little hunters, Bruce and me. (In reality, the owl poised no danger to us.) Among things, the owl could see very well at night, but he did not like sunlight and did most of his hunting at night. Look out little rodent!

So what did we "big hunters," led by Dad, do? We picked up red clay clods and pummeled the heck out of him. After about five minutes of hitting him, we felt we had showed him who was boss. Surely, he was hurt badly though he just would not move as we hit him. We drew tired of throwing clods, left Mr. Owl who probably died, and left with our chests popped up.

(Owls were probably not protected back then, but now humans know the owls are lauded for their balance of wild life and look upon owls as one of Nature's beautiful creatures. For that little venture Dad, Bruce and I stand cruel, shameful and stupid. Today we stand "sorry, Mother Nature.")

OUR DRIVE-IN ADVENTURES

There were TVs in Duncan, but they were few and far between! Then one day, a neighbor of ours who lived directly behind us across our alley got a TV. They talked about it and could see the longing in the eyes of two cute little boys, Bruce and me. A few weeks after they got it they asked us if we would like to come to their house at four PM on Sunday afternoons and watch the one-hour show, Hopalong Cassidy, (Hoppy's horse was Topper) sponsored by Wonder Bread. Yes! We were in "cowboy heaven." We saw Hoppy a month of Sundays!

One of America's newest crazes in the 1950's was Drive-In Movie Shows. Early on, Duncan had its own drive-in, the Chief Drive-In! They were packed almost every night. It was great fun and many times was car-full-for-one-dollar night. Mom used to pop a large sack full of popcorn. We took that and a couple of chilled two quart-size bottles of Vess soda. Usually root beer was fond of the whole family. It was not unusual for us load up with popcorn and soda pop and head for the drive-in at least twice a week and occasionally thrice.

Of course, the movies at the Drive-In did not start until it was dark, so the movies ran to after 11:00 each night. The show included reviews of coming attractions, one or two cartoons, finally the main feature. A lot of westerns were liked by all and a few full long cartoons. We saw all types of movies coming straight from Hollywood to our local Drive-In. We went a lot. The movie changed about three or four times a week, so it was not unusual to see the Cobb car "drive-in" two or three times a week. I remember "Bambi" as one of our favorites, and "Black Bart" with Dan Duryea. He was so smooth!

Dad was ingenuous and put together a device that could be mounted on the rear of the New Holland baler we had. The device would alert the tractor driver the twine was not knotting. That, of course, would replace "my job" in the rear. Dad neatly put together the device, complete with New Holland red paint. He sent it to New Holland. About two months later they sent him a letter telling him that such was not needed. A year later that innovation came out on the new model of hay baler. New Holland had lawyers; Dad did not, nor could he pay for one! Obviously there would be no suit!

By 1950, industry had converted from production of war materiel to civilian goods. New hay balers were for sale on the market and not a few farmers were borrowing money and investing in their own hay baler. Dad and his baling demand had waned, so he sought a new adventure of securing a job. He got a contact with someone who could use him as a car salesman. That would be in Chickasha with the Chevrolet Motor Company. There were two owners, one was seldom around so was sort of a silent partner. The other was Charlie Davis, an on-site owner.

However, there was a catch to the new job. The family was in Duncan and the job was in Chickasha. For a while Dad worked in Chickasha on Monday through Saturday at the car place. He drove home on Wednesday evenings and drove back to Chick Thursday morning. This was 40 miles and in those days took about an hour. He was home later Saturdays and left early Mondays. All the time Dad was looking for a home to rent in Chickasha and looking to sell our Duncan home and Dad's baling equipment.

With the baling equipment and Duncan home sold and a house

rented we were ready to move to Chickasha via U.S. Highway 81 through Marlow and Rush Springs. Rush Springs is called the "Watermelon Capital of the World." Nobody could argue that as they had some of the biggest dark green watermelons I had ever seen, and many a road side farmer's stand sold them for a great price. Sometimes for four or five for one dollar! I would bet that Rush Springs still call themselves "Watermelon Capital."

BACK TO CHICKASHA
ON 7TH STREET

Time passed several months and we moved to Chickasha. We were in a rental house across from the Catholic Church and school, and only about two blocks from "town."

In November 1951, we moved our furniture into a five room rent house on East 7th Street. We had a living room, dining room, kitchen, and two bedrooms plus a bathroom. The bath tub was funny as it seemed "old fashioned" with it legs on a large tub with big legs sitting on the floor.

It also had a garage behind the house with a dirt floor. I was playing in the dirt floor (boys love dirt!) one day and starting getting coins that obviously someone in the past had dropped them (probably one at a time over time) in the dirt. The coins were pennies, nickels and dimes. All were quite old as they featured Indian heads and they were dated in very late 1800s or early 1900s. (Hey folks, "we" were not long from the Indian Territory; we were in it!) One would think that they were keepers as antique coins. I was eleven, what was an "antique?" There was a local grocery store just a block and a half from our house. Bruce and I headed for the grocery store and traded them for candy. Boy, I would love to have those coins back now!

We visited that local grocery store many times to get Mom some need for the family; it was also on the way to our new school, West (Elementary) School. Besides West, Chickasha also had five other public and a Catholic elementary school.

GO WEST (SCHOOL), YOUNG MEN!

Bruce and I entered the elementary West School sometime in the fall of 1951. Bruce was in second grade and I was in Miss Potts' fifth grade class.

Remembering Valentine's Day as a fun event at each class in the school. Moms used to bring in sweet treats for the class. Each student used to decorate a paper bag and tape them around the blackboards. Then we would buy one cent Valentine cards for each other member of our class. Now, it there was a special young girl that you liked especially, she got a five cent card!

That Easter Mom or Dad or both got us dyed colored chicks. They did fine for about two months, but all died even though we thought we took good care of them. Guess they did not like the warm light bulb in their box. For several years in Chickasha, we each got a colored chick at Easter.

By the way, it's 1951 and we did not have television. But very few folks had TV. But we had the Hoppy (Cassidy) "bug".

Dad seldom put our car in the garage as the dirt was like talcum powder and easily found itself on the car. Like most all square blocks had an alley that ran through the middle of the block. Our alley ran right next to the house and was only about ten feet from the alley. So Dad conveniently pulled off of the alley onto the small back yard's thin grass and parked.

Those alley ways all over town were used to dump one's trash/garbage. Most folks used a 55 gallon steel barrel. I remember that we were allowed to "burn down" barrel and "had fun" with long sticks we cut from a tree.

After time (do not remember how long) some guy from the town (I think) came along and dumped the barrel. We used to have "fun" watching the maggots squirm. Nasty mean old things . . . I mean Bruce and me!

CRAZED (?) DOG

One day I was sent to the grocery store a couple of blocks away to get something Mom needed. On the way to the store there lived a dog. By himself he was okay. But this time he had a friend whose master was visiting kin folks. As soon as I came walking down the sidewalk, those two dogs came screaming, barking and growling toward me, such a nice little boy. Thought they would calm down as I stopped. Absolutely no stopping in those guys! The guest dog jumped at me with his mouth ready for action and took a two inch hunk of meat out of my left hamstring. I sprinted the last 60 yards to the store, and the man there hushed off the dogs and called Mom. I had no more bites as I ran so fast they never had a chance to jump onto me. Now that was fast!

I was bandaged. The police were there and took the "guest" dog and locked him up for 10 days which was the time required to be sure the animal did not have rabies. He passed which was good for me, as I heard all kinds of stories about how painful the rabies shots injected into the stomach area were and required about four or five shots. Kid and the dog both survived the encounter!

BOYS AND MOVIES IN CHICKASHA

We only went to a drive-in in Chickasha once and I really do not know why, but there were plenty of movie houses in Chick. That one drive-in movie was Burt Lancaster in From Here to Eternity; it was a great movie and garnered several Oscars. There were at least four movie theaters in town, the Washita, the Rialto, the Pix and one other. Early on we went to the Washita and the Rialto as they were the cleanest and showed the top movies. Bruce and I would once again go to the movies on Saturdays, when Mom had 40 cents.

Bruce and I did not care about "clean" so we eventually drifted toward the Pix movie theater. On Saturday, the Pix always had the fare we wanted: a cowboy movie, a cartoon and two serials. We just had to go every Saturday! One Saturday we were a little later than normal so Mom had to go in to find us. She found us and also three or four mice/rats. She declared that this establishment was too nasty for her cute little boys to habituate. Through the week, we whimpered and moaned until Mom relented and let us go the next Saturday as then was the finale of the serial playing there. Never again, Boys. Thank you, Mom. Good bye, Superman, Rocket Man, Flash Gordon, Buster Crabbe, Clyde Beatty and Pix mice/rats!

Now there were times that economic times dictated lean times for our family and we lived from pay check to pay check. Dad made $75 each two weeks with more if he had sold a car and/or truck. Once he sold a semi-trailer truck and he got a big commission; we were "rich!" That was the only time he sold such a truck. There were many bi-weekly checks with only that $75 and we had to scrape. Well, Mom and Dad had to scrape by, but we did not realize.

One Sunday, Bruce and I wanted to go to the movies, at the Rialto, think it was "Destination Moon". Mom and Dad could only scrape up 18 cents, after they searched in every "nook and cranny" for coins. But, wait. Several weeks ago, Teddy had been playing with coins and had stuck some into an interior door keyhole.

To help their cute little boys Mom used all types of "things" to jimmy those coins out of that keyhole. Finally, eureka! Two more cents! Mom and Dad were so-o-o happy to see their cute little boys go to the movies on Sunday afternoon. Off we were and walked the five blocks to the Rialto; no candy but we got in and saw the movie. Thank you, folks, for letting us go to the movies while Teddy took his nap.

[Years later, I realized why our parents were so glad to send us to the movies on that lazy Sunday afternoon while Teddy slept!]

With TV which at that time would be found in very, very few households so many of us got to go to the movies . . . 10 cents for children (12 and under) and 25 cents for adults; 35 cents for "big time" movies. We saw a lot of westerns . . . Roy Rogers (Trigger, his horse and Bullet, his dog) and Gene Autry (Champion, his horse) were still there. Dad liked them too and did not mind going with us. I remember "The Will Rogers Story", "Salome" in which Rita Hayworth danced for King Herod to get John the Baptist's head (she got it!), and "The Greatest Show on Earth" a circus story with Charlton Heston, Jimmy Stewart, Betty Hutton, and Cornell Wilde. Jimmy was a criminal who was a clown and always wore his grease paint clown face make-up to hid his identity; big train wreck in the end. Wow! Was that ever cool! The circus survived; boy, that was close!

In 1954, we went to the movie theater and saw what seemed to be the first well-shot of a movie as a horror movie. It was "The Creature from the Black Lagoon" and we all watched that movie on the seats of our edges, as it really got to us!

I remember a chum, call him Wendall, from West School who lived about a block from school and about three blocks from us on East 7th street. I recall someone probably his dad tied a large rope in a large tree in his backyard. The game was to have the guts to climb on top of their garage and swing off the roof with the rope and "live without killing yourself." We all did it, though a bit "hairy."

In 1952, Wendall's family bought a television. TV! A couple of times Wendall's mom invited us in to watch Flash Gordon on the small circular screen (about a dozen inches across). Of course, it was black and white; this one with a slightly greenish-yellow hue. But it was television! A few brief marvels of what the future had in store.

I had seen a few Black boys and men in Granny Bagby's area in Missouri but had only a few conversations with them. I remember this Black man in Chickasha used to drive his horse-drawn, rubber-tired wagon up and down the alleys and picked up garbage. I first saw this wagon-borne Black man at my friends, Wendall's alley way. I figured he would feed his hogs with it. Never any problem but at my age I really did not know much about the Black-White "tensions." [Later, of course, I would know and think how stupid we were.]

While we lived in Chickasha, Dad's sister Aunt Etha who had worked in an Elk City, OK dress shop for years, met a nice man, Ed Moss. He worked for the Federal Selective Service that ran draft boards throughout the state and his job was to review each county board's operation about twice a year. Obviously, he was on the road working all week, but was home on weekends. Mr. Moss and Aunt Etha got married and lived in Oklahoma City.

Mr. (now uncle) Moss always ate with us when he was working Grady County. He had a second job selling gadgets like key chains to promote businesses most with their logo and name on the gadget. Obviously, he had a lot of time with little to do when his day's work at the draft boards shutdown for the day. Bruce and I liked to see him, as he always gave us some little gadget that we thought were cool. Hey, we were just little guys!

DAD SPREADS OUT

Dad joined the Chickasha American Business Club (ABC Club). Probably did so because his boss Mr. Davis recommended it. Dad always had an out-going personally, so he got very involved in the club getting many of his ideas adopted by the membership.

There was a very accident-prone stretch of US Highway 81 north of Chickasha. It involved a slight curve and several fatalities had occurred there. Dad got the ABC Club to finance his project to have a large sign made with words and flashing red lights. After the sign was installed, accidents there were almost non-existence and by the time we leave Chickasha there had been no deaths there.

Because of Dad's many works, he was elected President of the Chickasha ABC club.

Dad's acquaintances led our family to join the Chickasha First Baptist Church. I remember a young family man named Bill Weller who owned a moving company and taught me in Sunday school. Mr. Weller was a friend of Dad from the ABC Club. I remember Vacation Bible School there and I was baptized there. I was a bit afraid as I was totaled dunked there as was the Baptist tradition. During one three month stretch in the local Baptist church people who attended every Sunday school session we got a special painted and kiln-fired plate. Our family got five of them.

The boys went to town with Mom once in a while when we needed new shoes, usually at C.R. Anthony's (may have been another shoe store). We loved going there, as they had a gizmo in which you could stick your foot and see how well the shoe fit. Looked like an X-ray that showed your shoe, foot flesh outline and the bones of your foot. Magic! We thought we were like Superman using X-ray vision. I swear it must have been using X-rays as we were exposing our body to intense X-rays. Somebody must have eventually realized that was dangerous; never saw such a gizmo again.

This was about the time that I began to be exposed to bad language, not from my folks but from playmates. Likely, they learned new "words" that folks tried not to pass around such words when kids were around. But kids were keenly aware when a word "slipped out." They catalogued them and then tried to expand the word and learn the meaning. I do not remember Mom and Dad curse much, maybe a "damn" or "shit" was it.

We learned grittier words from playmates. The "F" word made it to my vocabulary in the fifth grade. Mom heard me repeat "the" word and I did not really know "what I was talking about." She sat me down and in her words explained the "birds and bees" to me. Think Bruce was there too. We became "men of the world"! Sure?

It was several years to come before we became connoisseurs of teenager "potty- mouth" words. Boy, . . . we thought we were so cool and mature! Duh!

Something new is in town! A new ice cream stand, Dairy Queen, the rage of America and now we in Chickasha, Oklahoma had one. They only had two ice cream cones, one for 5 cent and another for 10 cents. They also had banana splits and chocolate and strawberry sundaes. Later, they had cones with chocolate or strawberry strips throughout the ice cream, such innovations! I bet that "Queen" gets rich!

BASEBALL IN CHICKASHA

Dad headed up a project at the Chevrolet in Chick. In Chickasha, there was little or no dependable wrecker service. He suggested the company buy a wrecker and put it into service. That would provide the community wrecker service and bring money to the company. Guess who drove the new wrecker? Tyrus R. Cobb was obvious with all his experience handling wrecks while on the Highway Patrol. On many nights Dad was on-call to wrecks. Dad had the wrecker with advertisements all over the wrecker for Mr. Davis' Chevrolet Company. Dad drove the wrecker everywhere for advertisements even to our little league baseball games and even had it in our team picture. You can see our entire family in our YMCA West School team picture: Dad manager; Mom score keeper; Bruce and me players; Teddy mascot; and Chevrolet Company wrecker!

Our town youth baseball leagues were run by the local YMCA. During WW II the Army had built a large hospital to care for soldiers returning from the war. The hospital included a bunch of barracks buildings. I remember a huge water tower was adjacent to the main building and talk was heard from everybody that a number of soldiers returned from the war with severe mental problems and several of them had climbed up the tower and jumped committing suicide. Evidence could be seen as the first 30 feet of the tower steel ladder had been cut off to prevent that way to jump. Most of the Army land and buildings was turned over to the town a few years after WWII.

Some folks rented the barracks to live in, as they re-configured the inside of the barracks for more comfortable family living. I remember a local high school coach (baseball for sure, likely other sports) and his family lived in one of those re-con barracks. Coach was Doc Lafever and had a real stud athlete son about three or four older than us. Funny remember was that Doc drank milk all the time; learned later it was for his stomach ulcers. How do I remember that? I have absolutely no idea!

Anyway the town and the YMCA benefitted from gifts from the federal government (probably like many other cities in America after WW II). Besides the buildings, one with a large gymnasium (with basketball court), several baseball fields came with the property. I remember at least three upon which I played. We used to ride our bikes (about a mile) in summer mornings and play "catch up" baseball all morning.

Chickasha had a class One-A professional baseball team. The young catcher of the team was a friend of the family as we used to buy shoes from him at store in town. Players did not make much money playing ball, so they had to supplement they salaries to live. Most even found a spare bedroom in some local's home in order to live.

Bruce and I usually went with Dad to the "knot-hole" club at the One-A baseball games. Knot-holes were a very common thing in the '50's where we actually stepped through a re-moved 2 x 12 board in the fence and had our own small stands to sit in about 30 feet beyond first base. The ABC Club sponsored the knot-hole club. A guest who was from the ABC Club chauffeured the knot-hollers? You guessed it, Ty Cobb. Dad was in everything and everywhere. Sounds like a politician. Hummm? Watch out later.

I remember one of my baseball teams when we played on the best of the three little league fields. Think we were sixth graders. Mr. Leonard was the coach/manager. He had a slightly lame leg, was short and wore glasses, but he was good. Mickey, his son, was left-handed and played 1st base and pitcher. Three other players I remember were Craig White, Rex McCarthy and Larry Zook. I played short stop and 2nd base. We played a couple of years together, no longer "school" teams. I was pretty good back then, but as I moved later into the middle teen ages others would pass my talent by, but I was still good looking of course . . . well.

My handsome Dad (seated left) as President of ABC in Chikasha, OK c.1954/55

West School Eagles (town youth baseball). Mom (left) & Dad (rt); me third left of standing players; Bruce second left of kneeling players and Ted sitting alone center on ground. Dad's wrecker.

WE MOVE TO TEXAS (STREET)

Mom and Dad were on the lookout for a house to buy for our own. They had a little money from sale of the baling equipment and sale of our Duncan home. Armed with that they purchased a new home in July of 1952 and we happily moved into a new home at 1322 Texas Street. This address kept us still inside the district area of West School though we were now six blocks away. Young boys would just have to build up their legs!

Young boys were disappointed to learn that the yard's Bermuda grass was still "infested" with those nasty tall grass-like stems that each had about 5 bards each on the end. The bards would "attack" and stick to bare feet, socks, any material cloth, and especially cotton (t-shirts). We sometimes would conduct "sticker fights" by pulling some of the stems up by the root, then throw them at other guys t-shirts.

Sometime before we moved to Texas Street, it actually may have been in Duncan, but an orange-bodied gasoline rotating blade mower appeared in my charge and that meant work. The lawn on 7th street was small, so mowing was quick and easy. The mower body was cast iron and painted orange and had to be started by a rope that pulled the motor fly wheel to start the engine. I had to fill the motor with gasoline and oil and secure the rope by tying it around the handle. Now do not let that blade cut your toes off!

The Texas street lawn was much larger, so it was a big job. Dad let me take the mower roaming around the neighborhood to seek employment. I tied our gasoline "can" to the mower; the can was actually a one-gallon glass jug that Dad procured from a drug store that used the jugs full of Coca-Cola syrup. I did not find much luck getting folks to part from their dollar bill. However, one nice man gave me two dollars. After the two hours it took, I was ready for a candy store run!

A guy named Tom Swinesford was our catcher and a heck of a batter. He was clearly the best player in the area. (Later, I understand he was a great athlete in high school and I believe he went on to the University of Oklahoma {OU}.) He was so competitive he would even explosively cry when he or we were not going well. Tom's whole family came to all the games. His little brother was John and his mother was Mary. The father, Darrel, was a professor in the Art Department at the Oklahoma College for Women in Chickasha. I remember watching him at our games craving some beautiful statures of Polynesian women and men in cedar wood. Beautiful! Some people are just naturally blessed with talent. Darrel truly was.

For two or three years after we had moved to Claremore, our mothers corresponded at Christmas and always sent us some of Darrell's work, ink block pictures of cowboys at work. One thing all of us thought one thing was strange. The two boys called their mother and father, Mary and Darrell. Guess new age a-coming?

MEET US IN ST. LOUIS

One summer we went to the Bagby's house outside Lilbourn. We were going to visit the grand folks, but our parents had additional plans. Being about three hours from St. Louis they planned to go to that fair city and attend a St. Louis Cardinals baseball game. They went and we kids stayed with Granny Bagby. They had a great time and brought us a couple pennants which we took home and proudly displayed them on our bedroom walls. Everybody thought those pennants were cool. You see, at that time the Cardinals were the <u>farthest west </u>professional baseball team in America, so everyone west of the Mississippi River were Cardinal fans. We kids wanted to be Stan Musial. Later our baseball hero would be Mickey Mantle because he was truly great and from Miami, Oklahoma.

Besides tornadoes, we learned to live with, but not like another strange weather phenomenon . . . dust storms. America's southwest suffered the dust storms of the Dust Bowl days and Oklahoma was right in the middle of it. While the worst of the Dust Bowl days were waning, the winds of the southwest still had a few dust days to keep farmers on their toes and not forgot to treat the land with kindness. I remember a two day long dust laden atmosphere when red dust enveloped Chickasha. There was no wind but the dust was suspended in the air for at least 500 feet in the altitude. We could breathe, but after a couple hours we would spit red phlegm. The red dust got into everything. Sleeping was very difficult as we had always slept with the windows open (no air conditioning) in those hot summer nights (as much at 85 degrees at 3 AM). We would hang wet towels in the opening of the windows. It did not help much and I woke up several times with my face in the window. (Our double bed was right against the wall under a window.) Fortunately we only suffered through a couple of those dust storms. Mom took hours to clean up the dust that had settled all through the house. I reckon the farmers were using good soil mechanic techniques at abating loss of soil to the dry winds. The techniques paid off, as today such dust storms are pretty much a thing of the past. Good riddance!

RUBBER GUN WARS

Almost all tires in those times had black rubber inner tubes. We cut out "rings" of the black rubber and used them with our "rubber guns." We sawed out an extra-long (about 18 inches) barreled wooden pistol "gun"; then we nailed a clothes pin on the "pistol" handle. Then we stretched the rubber ring and "fired' at targets and progressed to "rubber gun wars!"

Each of us sought a more powerful rubber gun. So we innovated. First, we stretched one of those rubber rings around the head of the clothes pin so it could hold on to an extra stretched "bullet" rubber ring. Then set we could shoot further and sting worse, as during the summer we went shirtless. Ouch!

We always looked for inner tubes made with red rubber because it would more easily stretch further. They were older inner tubes and hard to find, but when Dad found us one, we were loaded. Later we "developed" multi-shot rubber gun rifles. Usually they had three clothes pins mounted on the rifle, one on top and one on each side. They were then "fired" in reverse of loading. It was fun to sting other guys, but not fun to get stung!

Once Bruce and I were building something and we needed nails. I asked mom if I could ride my bike to town to buy 10 cents worth of nails. I have no idea where Bruce and I got the money, but, Mom said, "yes, be careful." I could not believe she would let me go; town was almost a mile and a half away and the hardware store was in the middle of the busiest part of downtown. I made it and moved up a couple of pegs in my "accomplishments" of growing to a man!

MISS CARRINGTON'S ELITE CLASS

I did well in fifth grade at West School and was also seen as a well behaved student, so I was placed in a special sixth grade class. There were only a dozen students who all did well and were behaved in fifth grade. This class was small (four boys and eight girls) in order that the teacher could also serve as West School's principal, Miss Carrington. She was pretty old, probably 60-65. I remember one afternoon after eating our sack lunches we started our afternoon class and Miss Carrington fell asleep at her desk. Being the behaving good group, we just sat there until she woke!

ORGANIZED FOOTBALL

That fall something new was installed in the sixth grade classes in the town. Football! Miss Carrington was the coach and we had five sets of equipment, shoulder pads and helmets. Somehow we got enough equipment to fit out the team and we played all the other town sixth grades. We had played in the yard for several years, but this was organized football!

There was another boy in the other West School sixth grade that I knew from recess, Charles Bentz. He was a bit taller than me and a bit better football player. Actually, a lot better than me! One of the strange things in life happened with Charles. Our summer before seventh grade, Charles' family moved. (A couple of years later when my family moved to Claremore, OK and I entered the ninth grade, there was Charles. He was on the football team in high school.)

In West School, Charles was on our team, as was I. Charles and I were about the same size. I was an average player, but Charles was really good.

When the West School football team went to another school to play I remember a bizarre play. West had one boy who was sixteen years old and was the tallest/biggest guy in our school; he was about 5' 10" tall. (He was old and tall not because he had failed school; he had to work to help his family for a couple of years and was now back in school.) Let us call him Jim Mills. He was playing defensive end. When a half back (3" 11"), on the other team came around end and there was Jim. The halfback was so startled he ran all the way to his team's end zone with Jim chasing him. We won!

CANDY MAN

Various types of candy or snacks always tried to catch our eyes to buy them. Our ready cash usually amounted to two or three cents so "penny candy" was the fare. There was a little package of four "square" "Kits" in chocolate, strawberry or banana and only cost a penny! Bought and ate a few of those. Then there were "Jaw Breakers" also a penny and dissolved very slowly in your mouth. Along came the York peppermint patty a chocolate treat which was like a small round candy bar. They were good but we did not buy many of them because they were two cents each. (Today, for the same York peppermint patty we pay 35 cent each or 3 for a dollar!)

Occasionally, we could buy for a nickel candy bar: Hersey bar (plain or nuts), Milky Way, Peanut Patty, or Bit-O-Honey. One neighborhood grocery store about a block from West School used to sell a little (about 2" high) cylindrical carton that contained salted red-skinned roasted peanuts. Now why would school aged kids buy those for a nickel? Well, you see the manufacturer placed real coins in some of the cartons. Nothing but peanuts was the usual, a few pennies (one each), an occasion nickel, and a seldom dime or rare quarter. So "we" taught the little darlings to gamble at a very young age!

One girl in Miss Carrington's class room at West School took a shine to me and I to her; must have been because she was about a head taller than me. Remember most girls at that age were taller than me. Hell! The whole world was taller than me. (Just wait five years.) Anyway, Karen Prague was smart and cute. I went to her house two or three times. She had a younger brother and he was a wise guy, but okay. I noticed that their "parents" seemed older than most parents of kids our age. Later, I learned that Karen and her brother had both been adopted. I had not known much about orphans but them seemed happy; that was nice. Junior High moved Karen and me in different classes.

Another girl in my sixth grade room was part Indian. Her cousin was a Marine in the battle for Pacific's Iwo Jima and he was one of the American flag raisers on Iwo Jima's Mount Suri Bacha. That picture was very well known and all of us had seen the picture several times. (We still see it in still and moving picture today.) She was a bit of a celebrity!

On many Sunday afternoons, we all mounted the family car and Dad liked to drive around town's neighborhoods to see what was going on and perhaps see a few folks we knew. We kids liked it, as we always saw other kids we knew and it was something to do, as football in the sticker lawn got boring for the five hundredth time or flying a kite.

LITTLE MONSTERS

Every summer there matured "tons" of cicadas which sang their tune and were all over our trees. We called them locusts, and we became hunters. We would grab them with our hands. They would flutter their wings when we grabbed them but they did not bite. When we felt "mean" we would shoot them out of trees with our BB-guns. We all would have jars full of live ones. The neatest thing about them was they came out of the ground as a pupa and would climb up the sides of trees and mature towards adulthood. They crawled out of their "shells" and left the shells stuck and dried onto the trees. We collected bunches of those "mean looking" shells.

Later learned these plentiful insects were named "seventeen-year locusts" or "cicadas." I guess they spent a long time in the ground before a short-lived summer vacation. In the south, they are called "thirteen-year locusts." I guess they liked Oklahoma because there were hordes there and I have only seen a few each summer here in North Carolina. They and their "singing" are neat. (Boy, they are in hordes this [2020] summer! Guess they do come out in plenty in special summers. Their loud "singing" started in the evenings around 8 PM.)

Mom started "singing a different song." It was Cobb time for Bruce and me to take up dish washing. I was charged as the dish washer and Bruce was in charge of drying those that I had washed. Folks, this job stuck in the laps of Bruce and me until we went to college!

Mom enrolled me into the YMCA Summer Camp program one summer that took place at the Shannon Springs Park (really nice place). We had games and crafts (whistle lanyards) and just free time to run around in the park and find ways to hurt oneself or get in trouble! The park had teeter tots, swings, monkey bars and another "ride" that I had never seen before (nor since). It was two heavy gondola-like seats on each end of a large arm that went way up and down and around on an axle. (Got the picture; hard to describe, but move on!) Anyway I had been riding in one of the gondolas and when I got off I moved out of the way too slowly and the other big gondola came down and crashed into my head. A whack, a gash and blood and blood! Others got me to the leader and they stopped the bleeding in about 30 minutes, but I went home with a rather big gash in my head. Mom declared me okay, and no doctor and no stiches.

Mom and Dad were both out-going folks and made friends easily and plentifully. Mom had her bridge group and Dad had his large group of friends in the ABC Club. Both had a lot of friends in the First Baptist Church. We went to a lot of picnics with their groups at Shannon Springs Park. The town swimming pool was there, as well as, a small zoo, picnic tables, a long wooden bridge that went across the lake, swings, teeter tots, and other rides. And an occasional "guest" appeared at picnics. Kids always found ways to rustle up a water moccasin!

SHORT HAIR AND CLEAN

Long hair was not in style for boys. Almost all of us had some style of short hair. If we did not sport some style of short hair, we were consisted to be a "hood." Okay, there were a few hoods around. Not gangsters, but hoods. All the Cobb boys had what were called "burrs" while others had what were called flat-tops. Both styles used "burr-stick" to "dress" our short haircuts. Basically the stick of "waxy material" had a consistency between a candle and Chap Stick. We all had burr-stick and would dress up our hair with the sticky stuff that made the hair stand up and was nice smelling. I guess the girls liked it because most of us wore the burr-stick. Heck, though it did not really smell nice, and it certainly was not cool to run ones fingers through a fellow's locks because they were sticky.

Now the hoods had locks and curls that the girls began to like. And loved them more when along came ELVIS!! No burr-stick needed there! Maybe Brill-Cream, the hair cream of the age!

Mom was for short hair and she kept her side of the deal—she would be the dealer of CLEAN! We boys (and our parents) never wore "dirty" clothes. Mom was a "wash and iron alcoholic." We always had clean clothes, even if they were old they would be clean and mended before we put them on, thanks to Mom. I remember Mom sitting under a lamp and mending holes in the toes of our socks.

And everything would see the bottom of a hot iron; it was electric but straight heat, no steam until much later. "Fine" clothes would get sprinkled with a soda pop bottle now filled with water and shaken through a special corked little nozzle that wetted the clothes before the application of the hot iron. Ironing was essential as most were made of cotton and they needed the tiny wrinkles ironed out. You see, 50-50 material was not manufactured yet; had to wait for the late 1950's/early 1960's. Goodness, remember Mom ironing most everything, even, sheets, pillow cases and handkerchiefs!

In high school, I remember I had two pairs of jeans (with rolled up pant legs); one pair got worn three days the other two days; every day always had a clean shirt of some kind. Mom was busy all week, but we were CLEAN!

Earlier when we first moved to Chickasha, Mom told me one day there was a war going on in Asia, South Korea to be specific. And things were not going so well there and US troops and those of the Korean forces were about to lose, but General MacArthur was doing better. Things got worse when the Chinese entered in the war on the side of the North Koreans. More troops were asked for the United States to provide them.

Oklahoma had a reserve division of infantrymen, the 45th Thunderbirds, their name from an Indian name. The division was called together and conducted training for a couple of months; the troops came from all over Oklahoma. The Cobb family was friends of several folks who were in the division and went to Korea. One was in particular of the Cobbs and we visited them several times as the division got ready to deploy. The family's father was a first lieutenant and fortunately he did well and was a captain when he came home.

One year we took advantage of school Christmas vacation, and the family drove to Elk City to visit Grandma Cobb (grandpa had passed away by this time). After a little talking I announced that I would stay with Grandma for several days. Mistake! Believe it or not, I was lonesome for Bruce! Grandma was nice, but I was bored after scaring all the birds in the neighborhood and then got a strange illness. Grandma's home was heated by open-faced gas fires. I guess the oxygen level of the home's inside was depleted enough to affect me as I seemed to always have a headache. I listened to the radio and liked hearing top tunes and even phoned in a request. Still "sick" though. ("Grandma, I loved you, but I did not love your home in the winter time.")

I was glad, when Charles (wife, Lillian), one of the renters of grandma's apartments drove me to El Reno, OK, and Dad picked me up there and we went home. Never loved home so much!

I really liked Charles and Lillian. They were a nice young couple. I thought Charles was a really cool guy, as he was a big roughneck in the oil fields and was a full-blood American Indian.

For years all of us boys had availed ourselves as a seat on the floor to listen to the parents' radio in their bedroom (the only radio in the house). We listened to such shows as "Fibber McGee and Molly," "Amos and Andy," "The Shadow," "The Jack Benny Show," and "Truth or Consequences." In the summer time, we even listened to such daytime serials (radio soap operas) as "Helen Trent."

TV COMES TO THE COBBS

Now, a "great" decision was made to move us into the future. Mom and Dad decided to purchase a television! It was a console with a picture about the 17 inch size. Of course, it was black and white. That's okay folks, we will never see colored television in our life-times. (You fools! Don't you know the fools are ingenious?)

In 1953, there was only one reachable station telecasting TV transmissions. That would be WKY-TV out of Oklahoma City. One station was okay; before we had none! As time passed a couple more stations began telecasting, but for the time we were WKY-TV and we loved it. There was one technical glitch. The signal from OKC was rather weak from that distance of 40-50 miles. We had an antenna on the roof like everyone. It was about 6 feet above the roof's highest point with the TV lead wire from there down into a front window of the house. Dad was always going up on the roof to turn the antenna to "seek" the strongest signal from OKC so the picture was best. Dad would call, "that better?" and Mom would yell back, "no", "a little better" and finally, "that's best." I guess you could say, that's "hide and seek" the signal! Network cable from New York was several years away.

Remember a fellow named Danny at WKY-TV who did everything on the air. He did news, weather and kids afternoon shows. He used to introduce a show that WKY got videos from bigger networks, called "Space Cadets." It was a fifteen minute serial three times a week. Also,

I remember the Oklahoma University football coach, Bud Wilkerson's 30 minute show once a week about goings-on at OU and tips on how to be a better athlete.

TV in our home was a big deal! The TV channel (initially we only had one, WKY-TV out of OK City) would "sign on" about 6:00 AM and "sign off" at 10:00 PM because they did not have many shows. When the station "signed off" the picture displayed the side view of an Indian chief until they signed back on. That would change in mid-50's when "the cable was coming" from New York arrived. Even then many shows were still recorded and we would see them a week late.

We eventually got some of the big networks' shows like Howdy Doodie and his crew: Buffalo Bob and Claribel, the clown, who warped into the famous Kaptain Kangaroo and his Mr. Green Jeans.

Because of the Oklahoma summer heat 95 to 110 degrees a lot of folks, including us, turned their TV set around and watched the shows outside through the window's "bug" screen. It was a great way to get kiddies to go to bed and many often fell asleep watching TV. Many neighbor kids would join us on the lawn. Watch out for those stickers!

Another group of viewers joined us as they liked to look at the light that the TV emitted. The ever glad crew to enjoy the TV light and rest on the bug screen – a hardy crew of June bugs!

Mom loved music so she was a permanent fan of Lucky Strike's sponsorship of "Your Hit Parade" that featured America's top seven songs each week. I remember the singers: Dorothy Collins, Giselle McKinsey, and Snooky Lanson. This was a very popular show. We had Ted Mack's Amateur Hour sponsored by Old Gold cigarettes, regular and king-sized; he had dancers costumed in large Old Gold packs, one girl in Regular pack and a lady in the King-sized pack. Cute!

Arthur Godfrey emceed his one hour variety show on Wednesday nights with songs and conversation; remember, the McGuire Sisters? Remember a Hawaiian lady who sang who he had met her there. I recall he had a lame leg from a plane accident and was "big" in aviation. Godfrey also had a one hour morning (10:00 AM) show five days a week with singers and talk.

My Mom and Dad both smoked 2 or 3 packs of Old Gold king-sized cigarettes every day each! I never smoked, but I bet my lungs were a bit tainted from all the smoke that must have habited in our house for years.

Dad never stopped improving things, but two enterprises stopped him. First, was an attempt at establishing a garden in our backyard. We all dug the ground in the designated garden plot and planted seeds. The ground was hard and when we dug it up it was dry and turned to "talcum powder." We tried to water the garden but to no avail; the Oklahoma heat just would not help us.

Then Dad decided he was going to drill, by hand, a water-well in our backyard. He borrowed a hand well-digger. It had a large bit with handle pieces about one inch around and the bit would dig a one foot hole into the earth. Work and work and the ground seemed to get harder and harder as we, mostly Dad, tried. Finally, even Dad gave up after we had a twenty foot deep hole and no water and the ground was rock hard.

Mom always found things to do for her little darlings, Bruce and Ty, attend classes to learn new and exciting things. One was learning to swim. We had taken swim lessons at the city pool, but Mom found that the local women's college in Chickasha was offering swimming lessons for youths. Bruce and I were really excited and when we entered the indoor pool at the college -- oh, the water was so clear and beautiful! Bruce and I were the first into the pool room and Bruce quickly leaped into the clear water pool and immediately he went to the bottom of the eight foot area of the pool! I was a little more timid and leaped only far enough to be able to hold onto the side. Ty to action! I reached for Bruce and was able grab him and pull to the side of the pool with me. [My first save?? At West Point, I was awarded a Water Safety

Instructor badge which included Lifeguard trained and much older – 47 years – gained YMCA Lifeguarding qualification in Salisbury, NC and actually making a save in the city pool by grabbing a swimmer by the arm after jumping into ten feet water. Good training in the Chickasha college pool!]

Once again, on Texas Street at Easter time Mom and Dad got each of us a colored chick. You know . . . I kind of think our parents liked the chicks too! This time we did something different and better. The chicks lived! They got too big for their box and began to jump out into the house. Hummm? We got a small bit of chicken wire (hey, they were "chickens" now) and built a small pen onto the back wall of the car porch that Dad had built. There goes that Dad of ours!

They, of course, got even bigger and their chick fuzzies changed in time to white feathers. These critters were soon full grown and too big for their pen. Naturally, Dad "knew somebody." A family just on the edge of town had a large chicken pen. We gave the chickens to them and we never saw them again. Likely, three fried chicken dinners soon adorned a picnic's fare!

MOM ENTERTAINS THE LADIES

Mom knew quite a few ladies and became a permanent member of two tables of bridge and Mom hosted them once every eight weeks. Mom always fixed refreshments for the ladies and her specialty was cherry pie which we all loved too. Not all the ladies eat the pies and coffee, so we always looked forward to the "left overs." She also had little bowls with candy and they had left overs too. There was more for the boys.

We boys, including Dad, had to be out of the house for about three hours. Dad always took us to a little cafe for burgers and/or hot dogs and a soda and Dad had his forever cup of coffee at 5 cents, then to the movies. [You know the other day when we were vacationing at Myrtle Beach, SC in a major chain hotel. I was at the breakfast buffet and without looking at the menu I asked for a cup of coffee. I got it and drank it. Gulp! It was a little pricey . . . 5 dollars!] Here we come . . . Gene Autry and his horse, Champion, with those cool little metal figurine guns on his bridle. Gene was also the best singing cowboy. Just ask Rudolph!

Dad never liked bridge, but he was onto dominoes! He almost always played with quests who visited our home. Especially, his brothers. I liked it because I was a quiz at multiplying by "fives," but not being an adult, I just watched. Dominoes and beer were usually the fare; no pie or candy.

COOL DANCING FEET

Mom had been a dancer when she was young, but I did not know how much. I remember Granny Bagby used to dance a little "gig" which was brief, cute and she liked to do it. Mom heard there was to be a ball room dance class for youngsters. Teacher was Mrs. Holtsapple. She was to hold classes on Saturday evenings in a large open room where dances were held during WW II. Sixth graders would have classes from 6PM to 7PM, seventh graders 7PM to 8PM then followed by eight graders 8PM to 9PM. I started when I was in sixth grade class. I really liked it, as she was a good teacher and there were GIRLS there!

I took for two years and learned a lot: the foxtrot, the Lindy, Samba, Mamba, and the Cha-Cha. The foxtrot (slow dance) and the Lindy (fast dance) were my favorites and best learned.

I wanted to take for a third year, but Mom told me that it did not look like we could afford it, but she would see about it. Mom took charge and met with Mrs. Holtsapple. Mom made a deal with her and I attended free. The classes were always short of boys. So I (now in eighth grade) was to go to sixth and seventh grade classes and then could participate in the eighth grade class. Wow! That was so cool. I loved it because by the time eighth class girls arrived, I knew all the new steps and was "Mr. Cool" on my feet. Mom, such a deal!

Dance on lady's for I am soon borne for the North. (Actually, north Oklahoma.) But not yet, as more is to come.

ON TO JUNIOR HIGH SCHOOL

In Chickasha, OK passing the sixth grade meant a significant change was in store for school borne children. While we still met each morning in our home room with our home room teacher, she usually did not teach us as we rotated from teacher to teacher for subject area, e.g., math, English, history and other topics. We were being trained for high school when we would not have a home room but had a locker in the halls where we kept our books.

I remember the "pants freedom" in junior high school years. The rumor had spread far and wide that "upper class" junior-highers would catch seventh graders sometime and take their pants off. Two boys lived with their mother (no father in sight) in a very little house about half a block from us on Texas Street. One boy was in eighth and one in ninth (he was big on the football team). When those guys started talking about "pants" I said, "If you do, I will tell your mom on you. I know her because we see her each time we go to the Safeway grocery market where she works." Not sure I scared them, but I never got "panted." I always kept my eyes peeled as I walked home my six blocks to Texas street.

It is possible that the boys' father could have been killed in WW II, as there always were families without fathers. In fact, the family mother straight across Texas Street from us had told my parents that her husband had been killed in the war. The mother raised two boys and two girls. Think the mother's mother also lived with them.

UNKNOWN, BUT SKILL BUILDING

I continued my football prowess (what a joke, but I loved it) in the seventh grade. I got a pair of men's football pants sized 40! Mom worked over those pants one weekend and by Monday's practice I could actually wear them. I actually made the number one punter on the 7-8 grade team. First game at Duncan, my kick went straight up; second punt missed my foot and I never punted again. Case of the nerves I think.

I also went out for baseball; did okay; got no greatness inspired by my great name. Sorry, Mr. Ty Cobb (first man elected to the Baseball Hall of Fame; to this date, he still holds the highest lifetime major league batting average of 0.366).

I did well in classes and was called on to recite many times. The girls really thought I was cool (at least I thought they thought that). Folks, this was the age where girls did that "maturity thing" -- three years before us boys. The girls were "after the boys" and boys did not seem to "know" that and did not care. Boy, were we stupid! A few boys knew more about the girls than most like me. I was an academic and a leader without knowing it.

Some teachers thought well of my academics and leadership, as they got me invited to the local Rotary Club to honor me for my school work. I went to lunch with them and was bestowed the "title" as a Yrator (Rotary spelled backwards). (Unknown at that time, but such awards would help me secure an appointment to West Point and its college education.)

I organized our home room basketball team which played at the YMCA. I even had the team meet at my house and practice. Dad, ever on the spot, had gerry-made a basketball goal. Practice was tough on hardened grass! Of note, I went on to score five two-point shots in our first game. Best I ever did. A one game wonder!

One thing that stuck mentally into my noggin during my "English" in the 7th grade was a short book about Will Rogers. (Interesting the first time the name Will Rogers flew through my brain was the new school I went to in Duncan . . . Will Rogers Elementary.) My English teacher had a brand new set of young people's biographies. For some reason (have not a clue) I chose the story of Will Rogers and I really liked and presented a short oral report on Mr. Rogers. In the 8th grade I saw the movie, "The Story of Will Rogers," with my entire family. So what? (Well, when we moved to Claremore, Oklahoma in the summer before 9th grade there was "Will Rogers Memorial." My new High School classmates were all busy building and decorating a Will Rogers float, as it was Will Rogers' birthday in Claremore, his home town. Hum, small world!)

[I think that was the last Will Rogers' day in Claremore as I do not remember ever seeing another. Could be wrong.]

I went on to surprises at the end of school year in seventh. During general assembly, I was announced to win two seventh grade award for best sportsmanship (think it was really an athletically award because besides the winter basketball home room team, I participated in football and baseball) and leadership (here I come West Point and did not even know what West Point or New York was!). I was not even in the assembly when I was announced as the teacher had me setting out cokes and cookies in our home room. Guess the teacher did not even know I had won. Someone found me and directed me to a door off the stage and here I was and I still did not know why I was needed. Surprise, surprise!

(I reckon I did not know it but I was molding myself to go to West Point one day. Being small, I guess I was trying to make myself "big" by doing things and being smart. Did not think I was smart as I had to study a lot to make good grades. Math came easy to me and that set the tone for other good grades.)

One girl took a shine to me. She made good grades too and wanted to be like me. She was Patsy Malone and about a head taller than me; most of the girls were taller than me! She wore glasses but was very pretty. She and her friend, Betty Ginn, did everything together.

KISSING IN THE BUSHES

One Friday evening, I was invited to a kids' party and it eventually became a kissing game. I was told to go into the "bushes" with Patsy. Right after "going into the bushes" a boy (think his name was James Nye) was sneaking up on us in the bushes. I was acting rough so I kicked hard into the bushes where it seemed the sneaker was and caught him square in his face. He was about twice as big as I, and he took after me and hit me square in the mouth with blood all over the place. Everyone came to my aid and things calmed now and by party's end James apologized as I continued to bleed!

Mom came to pick me up as the party was over, and I was able to hide my puffed lips and make it to bed without anyone noticing. At breakfast I had to tell the whole story and that was the end. Of course, my lips were still tell-told but that was life.

James did not have classes with me in the seventh grade, but we had shop class together in eighth grade. We were "poor" (okay, probably lower middle class) but as I thought, James was worse off than we. He informed me in shop one day that he had to go to reform school (Oklahoma's String Town) soon. Do not know what for but I truly felt for him.

Months later I was invited to a girl's Halloween party at the Chickasha Country Club. Costumes cost money so Mom went to work on her sewing machine. She took an old white sheet and made we a little baby outfit. It was like a full length pajama top with frilly shoulder cuffs, a bonnet with blue ribbon, a ten cent blue eye mask and a baby rattle. When the "parade" of costumes was conducted, guess who won the contest? Baby Ty!

BYE 7TH, HELLO 8TH

In the eighth grade for some reason I was in another group of students. It seemed that all the girls and boys in my home room were smart and as before we rotated together from class to class. (Patsy was not in my class, so she found another boyfriend.) I have some memories of eighth teachers. Mr. Shipley was science teacher. I remember he used to go the local slaughter house and bring a cow's lung and a cow's heart to "study." We used to have a paper tube and blew up the lung to see how a lung worked. I remember Mr. Shipley because he was also an assistant football coach.

I also went out for football in eighth grade. This included one week two-a-days for a week before school started. Grass was wet early in the morning and got muddy. Played some, but not much. Remember one day at after-school practice I was playing guard and got hit hard (as I was playing "second team"). I remember I spit out a large wad of blood and, man, I thought I had become a real football player. (Oh, how many wads of blood I spit out in high school.)

In the early 1950's, we looked much like players in a recent (c. 2015) movie starring George Clooney, entitled "Leather Helmets". We wore those same black leather helmets with no face guards and a single narrow elastic strap that went under your jaw and heavy "canvas" pants. The helmets had a foamy type of liner inside. (This type helmet would have never "passed" the NCAA today!)

My Aunt Bea (Mom's father's sister) had knitted a pair of silk "sweat" socks for Mom, as she had played tennis at one time. I wore the silk socks and had another pair of wool sweat socks over the silk socks; needed two pairs to make the cleats "fit" as no sizes available for this little Cobb fellow! After wearing the socks and a sweat shirt like jersey over shoulder pads at four or five practices home they went for a weekend washing and on for another week of practice. I wore out two or three pairs of the woolen socks, but the one silk pair was still there. Man, those silk worms were tough dudes!

In PE, we really did a lot of physical work on our bodies in eighth grade. In about the eighth month of the school year we were told that we would be taking tests to see how physical fit we were. We would do as many repetitions of various individual exercises (e.g., sit-ups and push-ups) as we could; we would get the year-end grade based on how many reps we could do. I did okay, but one guy, last named Goins, went "crazy" and did sit-ups for an hour and did 1,023 sit-ups. By the next day his abdominal muscles cramped for about five or six days and he had to walk around like a human "L" all of those days! Talk of the school!

During the time I was in the seventh grade Dad was in a sales competition to sell cars at the Chevrolet place. He did pretty well. He won a Frigidaire electric cooking range/oven; it was very modern compared to the old gas range we had for years. We thought we had entered the new age! We had this range for two years on Texas Street and moved it to Claremore, OK when we moved there. It was there for the next eight years I lived in Claremore and, as far as I recall, it was there for several years after I graduated from college.

I loved that electric cooking range because it came with a whole load of cooking recipes for cookies. You see, we loved sugar and we felt we did not get enough nickels and dimes to go to the local store and buy candy. But Mom let me practice cooking on the new range. Guess what I cooked? You got it . . . cookies because they tasted sweet. Another specialty treat was a recipe I found in Mom's recipe box was a great cake . . . Lazy Daisy Cake! Hummm, boy!

Dad won several other "smaller" things. One was a real nice six-ball, croquet set which we played and played and played in the backyard.

DAD FOR SHERIFF

Dad was well known in town as a very community sensitive citizen. He was President of the ABC Club, church going, and a youth coach. Many also knew that he had over six years as a State Highway Patrolman. Many people in the town felt that the county sheriff was involved in many semi-illegal or some illegal and they wanted it to stop. I do not know the particulars but many townspeople approached Dad to run for county sheriff in order to curtail the many unpopular activities in the county.

Many people who knew Dad supported Dad with funds to put together a campaign for Sheriff of Stephens County of Oklahoma. He was running against the current sheriff, Hitch Peron (not real name). That name, "Hitch," seems a little shady to me, but I was a seventh grader so what did I know. I know from what I heard from talk around other men when I was with Dad. He had a portable public address system and went all over the county (biggest in Oklahoma) and gave speeches all through the county on weekends. I went with Dad most of the time and I was proud of the things he said.

I was sure that what Dad stood for would cause him to win the voting, I believe in the early summer. Dad's numbers were high but lost in a very close election. I heard talk that Sheriff Peron's "lieutenants" had made sure than Peron got elected.

Our family was devastated! I remember crying. We thought Dad was perfect. Well, he was, but the system (Stephens County electorate and those running it were not perfect). At least Dad was told that there had been shenanigans carried on to assure Sheriff Peron was re-elected to assure that "goings on" could "go on." Hey, I was thirteen, what did I know? I only heard "talk."

(About 15 months later, we had moved to Claremore for Dad to "re-up" with the Highway Patrol in Claremore, OK. We heard from friends in Chickasha that sheriff was finally beaten in the next election and the shenanigans ended.)

Believe it was just after the sheriff's election that Dad decided to try selling cars at the local Dodge/Plymouth dealer's agency owned by Mr. Cliff Andrews, who I believe helped Dad in the election. Maybe more cars there would help the slow sales, really state-wise. Did not, so that was when Dad was starting to think about the Highway Patrol. We will see.

WATCH OUT FOR BICYCLES

One of my buddies was a tall guy (of course he was real tall compared to me) named Milburn Smith. One day after some late event, he offered to ride me home on his bicycle. Sure. He had me sit in front him sitting on the cross bar of the bicycle handles. "Jumpity, jumpity" we went about four blocks and did well until he hit a bump in the road. My right foot swung into the spinning front wheel spokes. Crash . . . both us on the ground with my right foot grinding in the spokes.

My foot was abraded and forth came blood. Somehow we got the blood stopped, but I was still a couple of blocks from home. Somehow I got home and told Mom that I think I was not going to be able to walk on the injured foot. She did not have much sympathy for me because to the dumb trip I had done on that bicycle, but borrowed a set of crutches from a friend.

Dad dropped me off at school the next day and I went without crutches. However, I had to hobble to classes all day and was a couple of minutes late that day. Several times I had to lean against the wall in the halls to rest as I would get pulsating pain in my foot. I lived! Never ever stick your foot (or hand) into a rotating bicycle wheel while it's moving!

Our history teacher (a lady but I cannot remember her name) used to tell us about the 1930's depression. She was a school teacher then and told us how people really hurt, losing their land, farms, homes, and businesses. She made more money ($75 a month) than most because she was employed; was not a lot of money, but she could make it. I remember the balding, glasses-wearing math teacher; everybody loved him (and taught us well.) Besides being a very nice man I do not remember any great new eureka moment for things math but he must have continued my math growth. And, Miss Montressa Wantland, was our Art teacher. She was so personally talented and taught us a lot of different areas of the art world. One project was painting a whiskey bottle; Dad made sure the bottle was empty before I got it!

TY COBB, JR., THE POLITICIAN

Near the end of eighth grade there was an announcement that the student body would have an election to elect the student body officers for the next year. I do not remember what caused me to run for Treasurer, but I did. All the kids running for an officer really got serious into the election. Many parents became pseudo campaign managers and spent a bit of money on posters and "business" cards ($5 for a 100) to hand out. We did not have the kind of money many folks were putting out for such. But Mom went to work!

She went to the dime store downtown and paid 20 cents for two packages of play money and a marker pen. Then she printed my name onto the play money bills in big black letters, "Ty Cobb for Treasurer" and those became my "business cards"! Everybody loved them and wanted one and I handed out 200. Pretty soon others did the same, but my Mom made me the first. She also took an older white dress shirt and took the marker pen to that shirt! She printed all sorts of slogans: "Honest Abe Ty Cobb"; "Your money is safe with Ty"; and on the front pocket she wrote "Ty Won't Pocket Your Money". My "business cards" and my "bill-board" shirt were the hit of the election. Of course, you knew it. I lost second to a pretty girl! (I can "see" her now, very pretty and a friend . . . name Simpson rings a bell after all these years.)

BACK WITH OKLAHOMA HIGHWAY PATROL

Really did not know why Dad and Mom decided cut loose from Chickasha and seek a new job for Dad. Probably several reasons, terribly upset by the sheriff election, there was some bad-talk going on by several cliques against Dad, and the economy for buying cars was depressed and it did not seem to have a real future for a family with three young sons.

No problem. Dad interviewed to seek re-instatement to the State Highway Patrol and he was hired.

In August 1954, our family moved to Claremore, Oklahoma, to live where Dad's new job back on Highway Patrol found us back in the same town where he started in 1936!

Being welcomed to Oklahoma summer heat was my most vivid memory as we rolled into Claremore. We hit there about mid-afternoon, and the temperature was 112 degrees, a normal August in Oklahoma. No biggie!

Dad had found us a small rent house on the east edge of Claremore (808 North Osage). The folks in the neighbor were nice and hard-working people. Most had three or four kids like us. Across the street were the Wheeler's. Buddy was my age and his brother Jackie was two years younger; Ken was older and was in the Navy. Mr. Wheeler was a carpenter and I believe Buddy's mom worked somewhere. Buddy was a superb all-around athlete, a football running back for sport, and football captain his senior year. Jackie was also a good athlete.

The Dicks lived next to us and the family had four kids: Billy was a year younger than I; Thelma was three years younger than I; and there was a younger boy and a younger girl. The mom was nice, loud and tall; an outdoors type woman, about six inches taller than her husband. He was a mason. They usually camped out to a nearby river each weekend and came home Sunday afternoon with a mess of big fish, usually carp. They cleaned them and canned them. They also showed up with a mess of bull frogs and fried their legs which tasted good. Tasted just like chicken!

Across from the Wheeler's on their other side were the Chambers. Raymond was a senior in high school; Bob was a year younger than I; Earl, Bruce's buddy, and same age; then a younger cute little girl and a boy (I am not sure if he was cute!). Mr. Chambers was a carpenter. Mrs. Chambers was a mother.

Beyond the small cow pasture behind us was the Woodson's and beyond them laid farm area. The Woodson boy, Layoid, a year older than I, would become the high school quarterback (and one day a preacher). What the heck is a "Layoid?" Nobody knew, so we all called him "Doodle!" He later married a very pretty girl from my class of 1958, Janice Gable.

With all the boys in the neighborhood a clod "fight" was always something to do in the lazy, hazy days of summer. Hey, we seldom had snow in which to have snow ball fights, so clods. We would stockpile clods in our "fort," say "go!" and we were on. We all got hit, but not too hurt unless one crashed into your "pretty" face, and off to momma.

SKIPPER HURT HIMSELF

We did not have a trash barrel, so we burned it on the ground of our front yard next to the road. One day our dog, Skipper, was rooting around and stepped on a sharp glass shard and cut off the pad (about three inches up from the ground) on one of his front legs. We bandaged it and Mom took Skipper to the vet. If we had not taken him, he would have bled to death. Dog, stay out of the trash burn spot!

Mom was in charge of getting us enrolled in school. Bruce and Ted were both entered in Claremont School as grades first through eighth were housed there. I was in Claremore High School 4 or 5 blocks from Claremont. That was important as the only town school cafeteria was at Claremont. We were off for lunch for one hour and I had to walk over there to eat. As I recall high school folks had to pay 35 cents; others 20 cents. That means we just got more beans. Actually, my favorite meal there was pinto beans with "flakes" of hamburger meat. We saw that meal about every sixth lunch. Not a gourmet meal but it was good for us, and 66 years later I still like it!

Interesting, one of the first things I remember about the second week of ninth grade high school was the big parade coming up to celebrate Will Rogers' birthday. He had always claimed his home was Claremore and become a world famous humorist and movie star. After he died in a plane crash, the Will Rogers Memorial was built in Claremore and has been well-visited since, as it sat right on US 66. (Then I remembered my introduction to Will when I lived in Duncan and Chickasha. I had chosen the biography of Mr. Rogers to read in the 7th grade, and once all the Cobbs had attended a great movie, The Will Rogers Story, starring Will Rogers, Jr. at the Chickasha Washita Theater.)

Watched the parade, but as I remember there never was another. Miss Gassett, math teacher, cited me in my yearbook for helping to decorate the high school float. Page in the '55 Yearbook tells me that

H-S float won grand prize. I will "pop my chest up" but I do not remember working on that first place float.

If right, maybe it was because Tyrus Raymond Cobb (famous baseball player) took "stage center." Nah.

Being about 5'1" and 98 pounds and seeing all the hulks walking the school halls, there was no way I would try football, though I loved it. So, I tried the next best activity, the Pep Club. Okay maybe Pep Club was about the tenth best manly activity in the school. All right, the twentieth manly best. Most members of the Pep Club were girls. Oh, that ain't all bad though! Had a few friends in the Pep Club, say Wanda Dale, Charlotte Copp, Sharon Sheldon, Harry Wingfield, Shirley Lewis and Caroline Abbott (her father was my dad's boss on OHP). Think my dad thought I should be Caroline's boyfriend? She was nice, but I fancied another girl.

A WEE GUY AMONG "GIANTS"

My mom was nice and bought me an official red and white Pep Club sweater-jacket to wear at school and at the football games. Cool, but sort of sissy for boys; I was hoping for a football letter jacket, if and when, I grew a lot more.

As a wee little boy in stature, I had experienced moving up to a bigger school building with lots of school mates from West Elementary School to 7-8-9 Chickasha Junior School, but Claremore High School (CHS) was a whale of a difference. These northeast Oklahoma dudes were mean, tough and BIG! Guys just looked at me and scared little ole me: Don Purkey, Don Woodson, Bill Ward (Chief), Harvey Hendrix, and Jimmy Summers (Meatball). I guess the other towns' teams had meaner and tougher players. Claremore's football season was 2-6. Gets better! I just kept out of people's way, studied hard and made a lot of A's in school, a whole lot of A's.

Making good grades got you noticed. I always met some upper class students in math and science classes. Not a few of them wanted to see what I was writing; some took sneaky peeks over my shoulder to see "what's happening." I did not cheat by passing notes, but "hey, I could not stop folks from gazing around."

Even in the freshman year there were not a few guys (even a couple of girls) who had cars and drove us over to the Claremont cafeteria for lunch. Other times we had to walk. If we got slowed at the cafeteria, we had to run to get back in the hour. There were a lot of guys who ate there, including several football players. Maybe because Carl Boyd, an all-conference senior lineman and co-captain, ate there; probably because his mother was a senior cook there. I remember her as a very nice lady.

Some of the times we had time to stop off at a little grocery store about half a block from Claremont. We would grab a quick sweet snack to top off our "gourmet" cafeteria lunch and chat with some girls who always hung around there. A lot of 5-cent transactions took place there for those treats or the 10-cent treats that some were more "healed" than most of us. I think some would take their lunch money and buy lunch at the grocery, e.g., potato chips, peanuts, Twinkies and such.

The grocery owners were an older (hell, when you are a teenagers a lot of folks are "old"!). They were most likely in their early '60s. They had to ride herd on the teenies at lunch time. Once I was showing off and reaching into the ice cream box, in front of the girls, of course. All of sudden the man grabbed me my by ear and escorted me outside. Did not hurt too badly, but I was embarrassed!

Most of the girls at the grocery were eighth grade. Guess they could not be seen with the rabble of under-class like little ole me, as they were about to be high school freshman next year! We teenagers were told that girls matured three years ahead of boys. Of course, we boys would have preferred it the other way! Aw shucks! But guys like me "chased" them all, . . ., usually with bad luck! Courting did not help us when most of the girls who were our age were taller than we.

Then . . ., one day a new girl and her family moved to Claremore, her father worked for the state highway department; his wife was a school teacher and I think he was an engineer for the state. Her name was Nancy Galbraith, and I was smitten! (That smit would last a long, long time!) On, for other things; I will "visit" Miss Galbraith later in more detail.

OUR OWN LINEBACKER OF MATH TEACHERS

Remembering my Chickasha eighth grade math teacher, . . ., then I met with the "linebacker" of math teachers, Miss Ester Gassett, a master of math from the University Oklahoma and you had better watch out, . . ., she was tough! Problem? She was tough, but she was really good. She wanted her students to learn MATH, and she would be on your case if you did not try. She produced several students who placed high at year-end math exams in the state. I became one of her better students, and loved it. I would end up with Miss Gassett all four years in high school math subjects.

Also, had a great science teacher, Mr. Harmon! With a college science teacher during WW II, he had served as an electrician on the Oakridge (Tennessee) Project to develop the Atomic Bomb. As a slow reader, I had to spend a lot of time on English and literature courses. Other subjects got their share of my time also. Time spent for all and still made a lot of A's.

Claremont Elementary School was about five blocks away and the High School was about ten blocks. Most of the time, we had to walk. Almost everybody did. Fortunately, school did not start until 9 AM (lunch 12 noon to 1 PM; classes back in session until 4 PM) each day, so students were like a bunch of "ants" heading to school. Mom or Dad would drive us quite a bit as Dad usually had a patrol car and Mom had the family car. Oh, yes, the high school employed four school buses to pick-up and take home some of the students. However, the buses were only used to take care of students out on the farms; one each bus serviced students to the north, one the south, one the east and one the west of town. So, all of us in Claremore's city limits had to find their own ways to make it to school.

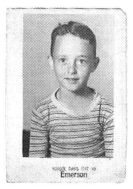

Me 2nd grade at
Emerson School, Duncan, OK
1947-48

Zebra H.S. - Senior
Guard

Me Will Rogers Emelemtary,
Duncan, OK 1950

My Senior HS picture 1958
(Marty Robbins)
"white sport coat and a pink
carnation"

FOUR PAYING JOBS IN CLAREMORE

We had our old bicycles, but we did not use them a lot, as seems abuse occasionally found our bikes. Our bicycles had another important mission.

Paper route! Yes, employment loomed in the future.

Bruce, now a seventh grader, was our bold entrepreneur who became an official "Claremore Progress" paper boy and was salivating for his "pay check." Bruce had to go to the print shop in downtown Claremore to get the papers, then fold them and head out to his route. Keep in mind that downtown Claremore was a good mile from our house and he had then to deliver about ninety papers every week day and Sunday morning. His was the largest route in town.

With such a large number of customers, I remember several times when Mom drove Bruce to town and through the route, especially on cold, snowy Sundays. Yes, we had a few "snowy" days in January/February. Even with Mom driving, it took about two hours to deliver all those papers.

After a few weeks, Bruce and I worked out an arrangement, . . ., I would be his assistant. Bruce got four dollars a week for his route, so my pay was <u>one dollar</u> a week from his four dollars. Does not sound like much, but that was the best job I had had! (Hay baling was the best job I ever had, but not when I became a teenager; I was broke.) Had those coins jingling in my pockets!

We had to go door-to-door once a month, usually at night, to collect for the paper we delivered. We were out to collect 90 cents for the month. (Today, my paper is one dollar each day and two dollars for Sunday compared to Claremore Progress for five daily papers and another on Sunday . . . such a deal in the realm of newspapers.) Occasionally, a few folks would give us a whole dollar and tell us to keep the change. Thank you, Big Spenders a ten cent bonus!

(A paper six days a week for 90 cents a month back then compared to today we pay one dollar a day for the delivered paper. Folks, that is 2500%.)

Some times on early Sunday mornings, Skipper got lose and followed us all the way to town and then, of course, accompanied us on the route. When he got home he took a morning nap as he had run about four miles to town and through the paper route and home. Good boy, rest well!

By the second semester, I was acquainted with several classmates like: Paul Akin, Jim Bevers, Gary Gault, Buddy Wheeler, Wanda Dale, Glenda Huneke, Nancy Whittenton, and Claud McClendon. Claud was a nice quiet lad who was a motorcycle want-to-be and rode to school aboard a black Cushman motor bike and usually wore black. Claud was a bit before his time, as Elvis Pressley was on the way about a year later. Elvis would become a sensation across American and onto the world.

Mr. Cline, one of our school's bus drivers, also taught a neat course on the History of Oklahoma. It was required for all freshmen. I thought it was cool to learn about the state in which we lived by our state schools. (I figured that every state required their high school freshmen to take a course on the history of their state, but was surprised to learn when I moved to North Carolina in 2005 that was not to be.) My freshman year courses, besides Oklahoma History, were Algebra I, English, General Science and PE. I went out for basketball, the B (or C) team.

DAD KNEW FISHIN' HOLES

Dad got to know a lot of folks in his work for the Highway Patrol, as most of their work was helping others, not arresting them! Many of those folks would let Dad fish on their livestock watering ponds, some of which were quite large. As Oklahoma was very hot and dry in the summer time and would often find itself in drought times. Wild animals were naturally attracted to the livestock watering ponds when droughts settled in. One such group that migrated to the ponds was SNAKES! When we went fishing, we had to always watch out for those critters.

One farmer told Dad the story that happened to a young Army soldier home on leave, who with a friend, ran down to their pond to go swimming. That summer Oklahoma had experienced a severe drought. The young lad ran into the water and immediately let out a screaming, "Stay out! Snakes!" He quickly succumbed. When rescuers got him out of the pond, his body was covered with water moccasin bites. When the pond was then drained, they recovered over 200 water moccasins.

The folk of Claremore many years before we moved there had intelligently thought that a good water supply for now and the future was a good idea. We thought this was a great decision, because we were part of the future! Plans were laid to dam up Dog Creek which was a "medium" sized creek from which folks would pull some good sized fish. However, the creek would become a torrent and flood much out of the creek bed. Such flood was, of course, an indication that creek could provide in time a great water supply. The Claremore folk took action and in a couple of years, . . ., voila -- Lake Claremore was ready for the Cobb boys to put their lines in the water to extract fish!

Claremore had enough water, save a calamity, for a long, long time. When the job was finished and Dog Creek had a few years to fill up the planned the lake's basin, the lake would have an eighteen mile shoreline with several large finger-lets fit for great fishing spots.

Initially, Dad chose to do our fishing on the north side of the first finger-let. I remember a large flat rock there from which we fished. However, in the spring when bass and crappies were spawning they were in the shallow water adjacent to the shore to lay their eggs. They were very active and would jump at almost any bait. We would catch some nice sized large-mouthed bass and crappies.

Some "commercial" fishermen pulled many very large catfish. The men had tied their catch on large tree limbs to show off their catch. They would cut the fishes bodies off to sell and leave their heads hanging in the trees. Some of those catfish heads would have had to have been once 60 to 70 pound catfish.

Dad loved to fish though I must admit we did not catch very many though we all had fun. Thanks, Dad. He began to take to several other finger-lets on both sides of the lake. Fun to adventure at the lake, but still there were not a great many of fish robbed from Lake Claremore!

The only folks who did well off of the Cobb fishermen were Jo and Bump who owned the nice bait shop right across the entrance to Lake Claremore. Remember putting a couple dozen "shiners" in our bait bucket and most of the time, Dad was good for a candy bar or two!

There was a small electricity generation plant below the lake's dam. (Surely that small plant cannot provide all the electricity for Claremore now.)

Though folks could not swim in the lake, there were many other activities that afforded from the lake. There were about a hundred picnic spots; many folks ran their motor boats on the lake; and on Independence Day there were hydro-craft races that went on all day. Those craft surely shook up the finny residents of the lake's water!

The most remembering boat trip onto Lake Claremore was afforded to me and a couple of other boys (one was Charles Lawhorn) who were in this older gentleman's ninth grade Sunday School class in the First Baptist Church. We found that our teacher was an avid sports motor boat driver. The teacher drove us all over the lake adventuring several of the many finger-inlets. The neatest small adventure took us all the way back to the place where Dog Creek flowed into the lake from the country side. We did not do any fishing, but we were promised the possibility in the future.

By the way. As I got a little older, I realized another activity the lake provided. At night, it provided several choice spots to park in a car for "making out" (kissing!). Every teenage at Claremore High knew of the pleasures of "lake kissin'!"

[About a dozen years later, I took my 5 year daughter, Christy, fishing on the first finger-let of Lake Claremore. She caught a fish!]

BACK TO WORK – SCHOOL!

I was not normally shy, but I kept quiet and did my work. I went to all the home football games and sat with the Pep Club in my red cotton jacket and cheered even though our team had a lot of loses. I studied well and long and made all A's my freshman year. I also went out for basketball and was on the B squad. Our high school only had one basketball court so the A team had one end and we had the other. I was not that good, so I got to sit and watch, but when I did get to play I had fun and, most of the time my buddies and I talked "about the world" whatever that means!?!

The Rogers County farmers hold a fair to display their ware each year in the summer. People enter a whole mess of contests and are looking to win blue ribbons for their efforts. Oh, nice apple pie – here's a blue ribbon! Nice calf—here's a blue ribbon. Oh, nice chicken – here's a red ribbon. This event goes on for a week and a carnival comes to town to set up rides to have fun. My Dad, as a State Patrolman, is given a mess of ride tickets, so Bruce and I hung around and rode and rode and rode on one machine, the Tilt-a-Whirl. The carny man got tired of us continuously riding that ride and only gave passes and no money. He decided he would fix us. He got the ride going real fast and kept making our basket turning in circle to the point we hollered "uncle." I was so dizzy I could hardly walk and my head was sick, sick, sick; think Bruce thought it was fun. Never again in my life have I ridden a Tilt-a-Whirl!

WE STOPPED POLIO!

One spring day in 1955 all the high school students were called to assemble in the new gymnasium that had just been built next to the main high school building. Some adult, probably Mr. McKeever (what a nice man), the principal, announced that a vaccine to stop polio had arrived and all of us were to take it. And, we did right there by swallowing a sugar cube laced with the vaccine. Polio done! Thank you, Doctor Salk.

ROSS GROCERY BECKONS

There was a neighborhood grocery store about two blocks from our house that Bruce and I were often sent to the store to get stuff for Mom. She even gave us a nickel or two once in a while. Unknowns to me, I was scoping out the place, for that store would one day become a big part of my teenage life.

Ross's Grocery was owned by Mr. Herbert and Mrs. Ross. Mr. Ross seldom worked the store, as he was also a city policeman. They had three grown children and one teenager still at home. By the way, the Ross's lived in the store building which was also their home which had a nice sized "quarters" area. Their teenage at home was Ted and was about thirteen. Mrs. Ross was the only one who really worked the store. She had a high school girl, Billie England, who worked there after school and weekends – store also open on Sundays which had a big business on that day as many places were closed on Sunday. Billie was two years ahead of me in school.

I have no idea how I got asked to start working at Ross Grocery. It could have been in the connection of my father and Mr. Ross as he surely knew my father since he had worked with the city police. It could have been Billie's connection as she was in the Pep Club. It could have been observation by Mrs. Ross as I shopped there. Anyway, at the end of my freshman year, she asked me to take a job there with her. Agreement was made that school was the most important and we would work out the details.

After working the newspaper with Bruce, my work schedule kept me from working with Bruce. Maybe he preferred it that way!?!

For me, I was into big money. I went from one dollar a week with Bruce to twenty-five cents an hour! Someday I might even be making thirty cents an hour if I did a good job. Oh, yes, I was authorized one soda pop a day. What a bonus!

IN CHARGE OF SPILLED MILK

Now what did the flunky at Ross Grocery do? Let's take a look at the "job description" say. It was easy. First, wait on customers. Then, everything else that needed to be done! Obviously, for customers, one had to make change after adding up the totals. Bag it. Be nice. And so forth.

We had a bit of everything. Breads, bottled soda, canned goods, candy, ice cream, large selection of cold cuts (many selections you cannot find today), milk, paper products, breakfast cereal, washing detergents, and a large selection of cigarettes.

Besides wait on customers many tasks accrued to a young teenager. That was me!

Almost every day one or two jobbers would deliver various things that needed to be price-marked and placed on display. We did not (nor did the big stores, e.g., Safeway) have in those days, UPCs [Universal Product Code] on each item you see today. Thus, I had to personally mark each item usually with a black crayoned pencil. That took a lot of time, plus placing the marked item in the proper area.

"Displays" required dusting every four or five days because we got a lot of dust from outside. You see, the parking area was right next to the store and was not paved. It was made of gravel and dirt! The store was not air conditioned so the selling area was not sealed to keep the dust somewhat down. We were "cooled" with a large floor fan. Many times you would find me leaning on the fan like I was dancing with that beast!

Cold cuts were a big item for the store "wares." We had to take a large "loaf" of the specific cold cut, like bologna, and slice it on the slicer, weigh it to determine the price then wrap it in white butcher paper. It got hectic when there were two or three customers waiting to get their selection. Watch those fingers, the slicer is very sharp.

As a neighborhood grocery, we had to have charge accounts. We had a little invoice book and we wrote every item and its price in that booklet and gave them a receipt. When there was only one clerk in the store at a given time, it got hectic because no other customers got any attention as writing things down took one's attention. We had about forty charge accounts. Most paid their balances every two weeks and others at the end of the month. You guessed it! Some but a very few, "forgot" to pay. Mrs. Ross was very kind with folks who had trouble keeping their debt paid at times. God bless her.

Another task that fell to me was attention to pop bottles which come to me by the hundreds. In those days, there were no soda pop in cans; there were a few brands of beer starting to be sold in steel cans. Aluminum cars would come later, but soda bottles by the hundred were there to be rounded up by "cowboy Ty."

Most of the bottles had tell-told syrup on them which made them a mess. Fortunately, the syrup was usually dried on the bottles but not always so it was up to me to clean those off. Then I had to place the bottles in the correct wooden case which held 24 bottles. I had to have them ready for the jobber to pick up the empties and deliver full ones. We had about five different jobbers with their fares, e.g., Coke, Pepsi and 7-Up. A full case of 12 ounce full bottles can get pretty heavy to handle. Guess that gave me exercise that probably helped me begin to tone my arm and back muscles for future football. I did experience a growth spurt in the second semester of my sophomore year. All those big guys who I feared in my freshman year heard about me and now were "shaking in their boots or cleats!" Yeah sure, . . .yuck, yuck!

Back to Ross Grocery . . ., because the worst task that fell to me was leaky milk cartons. Yes, we had put away milk bottles and moved into the modern day of wax-covered paper cartons! But, there was a not infrequent occasion when Mrs. Ross declared aloud, "we've got a leaker!" Those modern milk cartons did sometimes leak; the first problem was "which one?"

These cartons, quart and half-gallon sizes, were housed under the meat box on the bottom of the large, refrigerated display case which held our meat selection. The bottom held a large galvanized tray that held our thirty or forty milk cartons. The edge of that tray had a two inch high enclosure that held any milk that leaked onto the tray. That helped because the milk did not flow out of the tray into the display case, but we still had to find the leaker. We found the leaker by lifting every carton to determine the one or those whose weight was lower than normal. Hint: We were not beyond letting the leaker to leak several hours to help us identify the culprit.

The leaker found, we now had to clean up the spilled milk. This was one time when "you did care over spilled milk!" With a large basin of warm water, I pulled out each carton, wiped it off, set it aside, then clean up the spilled milk and replace the wiped down cartons. This occurred about once a week. Yuck!

DAD AND MOM SEEK NEW QUARTERS

Mom and Dad were on the look out to move us up a little in housing. They also had a little money from the sale of our house in Chickasha and wanted to buy or build a new home. They found a really new rent house near the new junior high school currently being built. It was about five walking blocks to my high school. It was to be a home that we would live in until a fellow built a new home for us.

About this time Mom and Dad found a rental house at 103 East 12th Street that they liked and we moved in there. After Bruce and I eyed the area, we noted a large house with a swimming pool in the backyard and on the corner of the block across the street was a church. We were told that was a holy-rolly church and many a night they would prove it. Now we were four blocks from Ross's store that I could walk, sometime Mom took me in the car or I rode my bike.

Bruce really loved a popular instrumental song and developed an urge to learn to play the song's lead instrument, the trumpet. The song was "Cherry Pink and Apple Blossom White." Bruce badgered our folks long and hard enough to get Mom and Dad to agree if he would join the junior high band. They did; Bruce did and he stayed in the band about two years. He learned to play that song but was not interested to staying in the band and went on to join the football team in high school.

The rent house was about the same sized as the house we first lived in at Claremore. Living room, bathroom, two bed rooms and a large kitchen in which our dinner table resided was our new abode. It was surrounded by mostly recently built houses. In the next door house was the prettiest freshman girl in my class, Sharon Sheldon. She had an older brother in the service and two younger brothers at home. A half a block away lived a family in a really nice, new home and there lived four sisters. Two years behind me was one of the four sisters, Dayna Butler, a very pretty young lady.

At that time I was sort of sparking on Dayna because you say a girl my age is not interested in guys her age, she was interested in guys two or three years older than me. Sorry, Sharon, I was always "cag-cag" over living so close to you. (By the way, I never saw Sharon after graduation, but someone told me that she was flying as a stewardess for a smaller air-line and became a real hero when her plane crashed and her did her job and saved several folks!)

As for Dayna, I was always sneaking around their house. I guess just to be obnoxious which is what boys do to get themselves noticed. Seems I somehow broke something on her bicycle and she told her dad. Guess it was not too bad, because I never heard any more about it. (But, about twenty-five years ago at a class reunion for my class, but who and several other ladies showed up was Dayna. As a teenager she was the "precious" attractive type looking. She was still attractive but had become an Okie lady type. She was about to get re-married and all she could talk about was how I damaged her bicycle. I think she liked me!)

MR. W.L. SAWYER

There was a couple living in a large home behind us; their "spread" took up half of the block on the other side of us. (Four houses on our side of the block; W. L. Sawyer and his Leona and one other house on their side of the block.) In addition was a large garage with two brand new El Dorado Cadillacs therein and a 40' x 20' in-ground swimming pool with a diving board and a nice bathhouse. I think there was one other residential in-ground pool in Claremore, but right there in our own backyard was the other!

I do not know how the Cobbs and the Sawyers got together but they did. Could have been W. L. noted that dad was a Highway Patrol officer or mom's friendly, out-going attitude meshed with Leona. Leona was also a nice out-going person. Before you know it, the Cobb boys were swimming in W. L.'s pool!

Mom was sure to control the Cobb boys in their use of W.L.'s pool as he and Leona were so nice to avail us of the pool. We realized why Mom was controlling how we swam and we were on our best behavior. It was like our behavior could be redeemed for "passes" to the pool!

Bruce and I were enlisted several times to help W.L. maintain needs of the pool, especially cleaning the pool. You see, the pool had no pump to circulate cleansing chemicals into the water. The chemicals were mixed in a large bucket and they were simply thrown into the pool. This kept algae and the like from getting too "dirty."

However, by middle summer the algae and the like won the battle for control of the water and the pool, so it had to be pumped out and cleaned which took about three days. No swimming! W.L. used a portable pump and just pumped the water out onto his lawn and onto the street for drainage; this was not harmful as it was principally H20!

Here come the boys! While the pump took about 30 hours we just watched our swimming hole leave us. Then it was time for the boys to go to work. The pool walls and bottom were a bit dirty and algae remained on walls and bottom. Bruce and I were given scrub brushes and hoses to do our clean up. This took a day and now the pool was ready to re-fill.

The pool had two, one-inch water pipes that would <u>ever slowly</u> fill the pool once the valves were turned on. A lot of water was required to fill the pool; using one-inch pipes took at least 24 hours to re-claim our swimming hole. Bruce and I got to be the first ones (remember workers) enter the pool. It was then without chemicals and was beautiful to swim in crystal clear water.

I remember visiting the Sawyer's home once in a den and W.L. had <u>THE calendar</u> of the time -- it was the original nude calendar of Marilyn Monroe! A 15 year old was "taken-in" by the picture. She was beautiful and really nude! (I wish I had that calendar today. I bet it would sell at a high price, and she was also good to look at! Poor Marilyn.)

W.L. liked to set up and check on a "trout line." He drove over country dirt roads in his Cadillac, at a "good" speed, but that Caddy just seemed to float! He took us (Dad, Bruce and I) to a spot in the Verdigris River just south of Claremore. The four of us strung a heavy line across the river where the water was shallow. Then we attached fish hooks onto the line by short leaders. On our way to the river W.L. stopped at a slaughter house where he picked up a bucket full of chicken guts and they became our bait. Now with a couple dozen of hooks were ready to invite our quarry. (Yes, that nice caddy smelled yucky as we drove the bait to the river.)

What was next? The night summer was warm and we headed for the river about 9 PM. Wading in the water, times up to our shoulders but about half of the hooks yielded us a fish! Oh, yeah, we ran into a big snake in the afternoon, but he did not want us, he had grabbed a small rodent and headed back for the woods.

W.L. took us all to a huge lake in northeast Oklahoma built by damming up several streams and a river, Lake Fort Gibson, where he kept his cabin cruiser boat. It would hold about a dozen folks. We fished, sunned and drove around and just looked at nature. Once we went there and got into some very high waves when a storm came up and we were truly scared, but "Captain" W.L. easily brought us through.

W.L. was obviously a person of means. He started young to work hard and soon had a small "oil" company that hauled and sold "no brand" gasoline to small independent filling stations. Eventually, he also had three or four small filling stations that sold the fuels he was hauling. And he made a good living with honest, hard work doing most of the work required for his company. About a year after we were friends, he decided to build an independent motel across from one of his filling stations and about a mile from the recently opened Will Rogers Turnpike. (There's that name again. . . . hey, Will.)

W.L. Sawyer (I never knew what W.L. was for; as a youth to me, he was Mr. Sawyer) a quiet, nice, hard-working man of Oklahoma!

COBB GROWS

I met and became pals with a half-breed American Indian and we did a lot of things together, especially walk to and from school. About a year later we moved to a new home but we got older and I could drive then; we double-dated two local girls who attended a Catholic high school in Tulsa.

He was Paul Moore who was about 6 feet 3 inches tall, so we resembled "Mutt and Jeff"! His mother was a nice American Indian woman and his father was a nice carpenter. Paul was a year behind me and was in the band. He played the tuba; probably because he was the only one big enough! His junior year he came out for football, but he did not like it and quit. He was still my pal. (And I heard he went out for football his senior year; goodness, Paul had to be one of the biggest ever lineman from Claremore!

TESTING OKLAHOMA'S BEST

The state of Oklahoma education folks held a day to assemble the state's "smartest" to see how the students and their town teachers are doing. In late April, students were invited to gather at the state college in Edmund, Oklahoma and tackle an examination that lasted about an hour to see who would finish first, second and third on the exam.

My high school sent a lot of students in various subjects; I was one in freshman General Science. First, second or third taken by young Tyrus Cobb in General Science? Afraid not, but I felt that by competing I learned about procedures and what the tests looked like. Should I be able to be selected by my teachers for future competitions I would be "ahead" of the "game." By the way, a senior from my school, Doug Anderson, won second place in the state senior level mathematics examination. Miss Gassett, the "linebacker math teacher," was very pleased, and Doug had been chosen to enter, as a "plebe" cadet, to the United States Military Academy at West Point that taught a world of math. Very interesting! Read on.

I played town league regulation-distance baseball and enjoyed it that summer. Unfortunately, I was not born to be a great baseball player like my namesake – Ty Cobb, The Georgia Peach, and a major league baseball immortal.

High School was in session in late August 1955 and, of course, I had a few subjects/teachers: English, Plane Geometry with the "Math Linebacker", Biology, and Driver's Education. And that new girl, the one I first saw when her family moved to Claremore. Then she was in eight grade and became one of the lunch time teeny-bopper girls at Claremont School where the only cafeteria was at that time. She was the one who had smittened me. She was now a freshman; in my high school!

I sort of thought I was "big man on campus" as I was getting a lot of rides to the cafeteria for lunch. Harvey Hendrix, Bill Boyd and Ed Vierheller all seniors let me ride with them when they were eating at Claremont. Harvey had earlier "scared" me as he was a tough looking football player (but he was a real nice guy); Bill was younger brother of Carl Boyd (graduated); and Ed was big in Future Farmers and was vice president of his class. I remember Ed always bought a cigar, a Mississippi Crook, to smoke after lunch. I fantasied about becoming a pharmacist and helping Ed with his farming financials. Wow! Dah!

By that summer, I was an old hand at the Ross Grocery at which we were very busy in the summer. We were especially busy on weekends as a lot of folks went to Lake Claremore to recreate! Sodas, breads, meats, cookies and a few others were the fares for summer eating fun.

When I began there I was the third or was it the fourth in the "pecking order" in Ross Grocery members. Maybe it was fifth, counting Mr. Ross! Anyway I met a fellow clerk, Billie England. Guess the father had wanted a son, because Billie was a girl! We worked well together and had a lot of fun, as long as I cleaned up any messes. Billie noted her opinion in my 1955 annual (book). (She said, "You're so darn mean you hurt! I hope you grow out of it. Anyway you're kind of likable.") Wow! She loves me too! Nah. She was just nice. In fact, I believe she was to marry Don Ross, Mrs. Ross's son, now a junior in college.

CLAREMORE GOES TO CHICAGO

I had a rendezvous the Windy City, Chicago. The school system assembled together a trip to Chicago for students. Mrs. Ross told me she would pay for my trip if I would accompany he youngest son, Ted, who was thirteen. Yes, ma'am, I am your man!

That summer Claremore teenagers loaded upon a passenger train and off we went to Chicago late on a Friday afternoon. We all talked and talked some more, watched the country parade by our train, then slept as good as possible in the passenger seats. Hey, we managed!

Chicago was naturally a city of really tall buildings. As we rode our buses, we gawked at the buildings; not many tall buildings in Claremore. We went to several museums and museum-like places. One place was the neatest place we visited, the (captured) German submarine that was at one place with the sub outside mounted on large pillars. It had been forced to surface by the US Navy during WWII in the Atlantic.

How in the world did a German submarine show up in Chicago?

I reckon the Navy got it there first floating it into the Saint Lawrence Seaway on into the Great Lakes and carefully slid it onto Chicago's shore from Lake Michigan.

After touring the area of Chicago, the students and chaperons loaded onto the train late on Saturday evening and off the train headed for Claremore, arriving there Sunday by midday. Good trip, but I learned I preferred little old Claremore to big old Chicago. Hey, we were mostly hay-seeds!

The long, hot summer continued in our home on 12th Street, as we were in W.L.'s swimming pool and I was working at Ross Grocery. Hey, somebody has to clean up the spilled, spoiled milk! The store had no air conditioner, as did most residences; fans were found in most homes. Most nights would find us sleeping with just our underwear shorts and we would wet our chests with water and lay under the fan breeze. That worked for about ten minutes!

Ours was a rental and occasionally some repairs or remodeling were improvements, and Bruce and I got into a mean fight. How were these two events connected? First, I yield to Bruce as the best fighter of us two. He was just tougher. Some workers had left a pile of 4' x 8' dry wall sheets in the garage of our house. I had some medal on a chain around my neck, and over something that brothers quarrel about we started fighting in the garage, and I had Bruce on his back on top of the pile of sheet rock. Bruce reached hold of the chain, broke it and pulled it away. I went crazy when he did that and, I pummeled him furiously with both fists, and he was in trouble until Mom came and pulled me off him. He said that was the only time I ever bested him. Brothers will be brothers!

INTEGRATION COMES TO CLAREMORE

In 1955, the teenagers of Claremore were in for a little shock . . . federal laws in America directed that all schools were to be integrated allowing

Black children to join with Whites in the pursuit of education . . . together. There had been a lot of trouble, especially in the South, and the folks of Claremore wondered how the teenagers would take that. Hey! Outside world, . . . the kids of Claremore took it admirably with almost no problem! In the entire high school there would be about twenty-five Black teenagers. Do not forget that we also had about the same number of Native Americans . . . this was Indian Territory. Again, no problem. Two or three Black boys joined the football team who helped the team well and the school freshmen class elected a young Black boy, Curmon Kelly, class president in a tight race with Fred (Corky) Williams who had been an early favorite. There were a few snickers. {Today such would be normal; thank the Lord.}

One day at school in my math class with Miss Gassett, remember the "line backer" math teacher from Oklahoma University (OU) was querying the class as we worked problems to turn in. She was also student advisor for college admission, and casually said, "Is anybody interested in going to West Point?"

A senior (me then a freshman) from our school had gone to West Point after graduation and I had remembered seeing a short subject movie in a Duncan movie theater on West Point that accompanied a full movie, probably a Tarzan movie.

I thought about it, as admission to West Point also included full ride financially as I was not sure my family could afford college. So I raised my hand and Miss Gassett gave me a brochure on the institute, and I showed my folks. They were both pleased, and I was on my way but had a lot of work to realize going to West Point.

OUR NEW HOME

Mom and Dad were also busy planning a house of our own and they were looking at some lots on the north edge of Claremore to build. A man by the name of Moffitt had purchased a tract of land and had sub-divided the sub-division into about thirty lots, built tract roads and put lots up for sale. Mr. Moffitt had built himself a house there, as well four or five other houses. Dad contracted a man (by the name of Burgess) to build us a house at 1329 North Dorothy. It was on a "slab" foundation with the interior layout like our home in Chickasha on Texas Street. I always thought there were some hot discussions between our parents and the contractor. But, the home was finished in November 1955 and one major fault would be found in the construction.

The house had a huge living room/dining room, a large kitchen, a bathroom and two bedrooms. The largest bedroom was for us three boys. Bruce and I slept on a double bed and Teddy was on a roll-around twin bed. One side of Ted's bed was against the outside wall where two three-inch wheels were resting next to the wall.

When we went to bed after a few minutes we would hear a creaking/cracking sound. Since we were in a new home and felt such would happen as the house "settled down." After a couple of weeks and we still heard such sounds, we told Dad and he could not find the reason. This went on for a couple more months and no relief.

Finally, Teddy noticed that the wheels of his bed had "broken through" the thin vinyl tiles on our concrete floor and had settled down into the space on the outside of the slab. Obviously, the concrete had not completely filled the slab. The weight of Teddy's bed breaking through the tile was what we had heard for several months. Mystery solved. Way to go, Teddy!

The outside interior tiles had to be pried up and the void there carefully filled with fresh concrete. We then slept without the "ghosts of Cobb's house!"

Moving to our new home took us to the north edge of Claremore which, of course, also took us further from school; the high school was a good mile away; more walking. I used to walk to and from school with Paul Moore, a sidekick from the 12ᵗʰ Street, when we walked together many times. Now I would walk with him to 12ᵗʰ Street area, then I continued on to Dorothy alone. Bruce had to hoof it to the new junior high school near where we had lived on 12ᵗʰ Street and eventually to the high school and even for Teddy later.

Our family doctor, Dr. Melinder, had four daughters and the oldest was a year younger than me. Humm? Dad was very friendly with the doctor and somehow I was set up with Marlene, the eldest, to escort her to a Christmas time formal dance at Cascia Hall Catholic, a school in Tulsa. Mrs. Melinder would drive us to and from the dance in one of her Cadillacs. The afternoon of the dance I bathed and got all "cleaned up." About ninety minutes before I was to be picked up I stood in front of the bathroom mirror and checked myself out. I had never shaved before as I only had "peach fuzz". Humm. "That fuzz is getting dark and really should be cut. Yep. It is time."

Grabbed Dad's safety razor, lathered up and stroked the first cut; I did not cut much fuzz, but I cut off a nice piece of my right upper lip. And, here came the blood! Mom, help! After chewing me out, she stopped the blood and administered some of her flesh-colored make-up to my lip. That helped a lot, but "Mr. Lip" was still seen by everybody. I made it through the dance, but my cut lip graced the ball! Beside the cut lip, I have to admit I was a bit intimidated. (I also proved a "safety" razor was <u>not</u> safe!)

CLAREMORE'S VERY OWN TEEN TOWN

Big deal had been granted to the teenagers of Claremore (during the latter of my sophomore year, let's say middle February 1956). The nice local members of the Veterans of Foreign Wars (VFW) had opened their building on Saturdays (then it was 6PM to midnight) as a "Teen Town." Not only did they open their building but agree to supervise it which was required by the town folks including the police (of course). That was a great new adventure for our town! Think we had to pay a dollar for a whole year's dues to help running of the building and buying new ping-pong balls! The building had a 40' by 40' dance floor, a large room with two ping-pong tables, and a small refreshments (primarily sodas) room.

The dance floor had a large juke box which had a good selection of the latest hit records the came to us from teen "kingdom" (think Elvis, Little Richard, Chuck Berry, Everly Brothers, Pat Boone, Fats Domino, the Platters, Jerry Lee Lewis, Bill Haley and the Comets, and others). The walls of the dance room were lined with folding chairs. The "ping-pongers" of Teen Town (TT) were in heaven!

The first night TT opened it was rather crowded but that was all right as it was THE place to be in Claremore on Saturday night. The first night, a true event for teeners, was going to be a little more dressy dance than subsequent Saturdays. Remembering my dance etiquette from my earlier Chickasha ballroom dancing lessons and knowing that a certain young lady mentioned earlier, Nancy Galbraith, would very likely be there, I asked Mom what I should do about that. Mom said let us get her a wrist corsage; so, we did. She was coming with a small herd of 9th grade girls she had "run with" since she moved here. I took the corsage to the dance and gave it to her, but perhaps both of us were a little timid; she was the only girl with a corsage there. Worse, . . . all of the older boys mobbed the young girls. I became "second fiddle" at the dance. Oh well, maybe she would remember me for a while.

There was another group of Philadelphia teenagers who were making a smash hit on America's television show on American Bandstand with Dick Clark. Here were teenagers making themselves "idols" to America's "teen-dom" and I was a member of that "dom." The Philadelphia crew showed millions of teens how to dance the new dances and Dick was introducing singing individuals and groups that all American fans only heard on the radio. We got them an hour each week day after school time.

I was a crazed teenager then. {Still am!} Claremore had a record shop, "Bunny's Record Shop," that most always had the latest record releases. The owner, Bunny, was not always in the shop, as his main job was a route where he upgraded all the juke boxes in the county. However, he was most always in the shop on Saturdays. I traded my hard owned money for 95 cents for a platter. My number one singer was ELVIS and I would eventually have forty-one 45 rpm records by Elvis. Also loved: the Platters; Chuck Berry; Fats Domino; Bill Haley and the Comets; the Everly Brothers; shall I go on? No, enough!

One day when I got old enough to drive I would have the girls dreaming to date with me. In the meantime, I would just have to rely on Mom to taxi me to TT. Would I last long enough to get to late June? I did, and it was better.

Things were changing at Ross Grocery. In the spring of 1956, Mrs. Ross hired a high school junior, Shirley Lewis, as an additional clerk. I really do not know why but I had been talking a lot about going out for football in the summer/ fall (I would be a junior) as I had been growing. Perhaps because I had eaten a lot of stolen (joke) candy bars! I was now 5' 10" and weighted about 150 pounds. Also, wrestling around those soda cases of twenty-four full or empty, could not have but helped build up my shoulders a little. By my opinion, I finally got big enough to give it a shot.

Shirley and I got along famously. Hey, she was cute and shy. And I was well versed in grocery business things! Mr. Ross liked seeing her around and he teased her a lot. Of course, I was still the clerk that had to tend to spilled, spoiled milk and tend of the soda pop bottles, full and empties. Shirley's boyfriend would usually pick her up after work and always came in for ten or fifteen minutes before she was off. Think he was placing in everybody's mind that Shirley was his! Think Shirley's beau was Lewis Stephens in the same class (juniors).

Just about things "settled down" at Ross Grocery, a huge change for all occurred. The Rosses sold the grocery to a man and his wife. They were a younger (probably late thirties) couple and the man, Hershel, had grocery experience and was a butcher. The wife (do not remember her name) was a second wife, a very pretty lady with a friendly personality that made a nice additional to the staff. Fortunately, they kept Shirley and me on as staff.

They also constructed a major additional onto the store which doubled it in size and Hershel purchased a butcher block so he could prepare more meats to the fare of our refrigerator case. I got to now clean the butcher block, but Hershel also taught me how to cut up a whole chicken the butcher way. A new talent for the store, but pay remained the same.

I continued to spend a lot of time with my studies for high school subjects (English, Biology, Plane Geometry, American Literature, and Driver's Education). Besides doing well in the subjects' requirements I was really working "it" landing good attendance; remember not being out of school helped in challenging passing final exams. I once again made all "A's" and the Oklahoma Honor Society.

Town summer baseball visited us with me at fifteen and the last year for town ball; one at sixteen morphed to American Legion baseball. I knew that the Legion ballers could do without my talents. Ty Cobb has met his end. So I was determined to make the best of it and have fun. With about three games left in the season one night, the coach came to me with a situation. Seems our catcher was on vacation and he wanted me to catch. Told the coach I had never been a catcher and I really did not know how. He was to give me a personal tutorial on catching; we had <u>about an hour before game time.</u>

The coach showed me how to properly wear the equipment. (Note that, in 1955, there was no such thing as a catcher's helmet which came about 15 years later. And, I remember that the catcher on my town baseball team in Chickasha had moved too close to the home plate and when the opposing batter took a big swing at an incoming ball he hit the back of his head with a bat. Yes, deep cut and blood resulted to our catcher. Fortunately, the catcher acted like he was cool once the blood was stopped.) So, I positioned myself well back from the batter's position. As the game progressed I did sneak a little closer to the home plate.

The coach told me to try to shake-up batters by talking and razing them. [Nobody has ever told me that I was quiet and that I did not talk a lot.] So, I got to "work" and really let the batters "have it." Mom later told me it was a little embarrassing and that folks in the bleachers heard me well! Several batters told me to "shut up!" And, my coach loved it and thought it was worth it. So it continued, "Swing!" "Hey, batter, batter." "You missed that beauty!" "Here comes his best fast ball!" A couple of batters got so flustered they knocked the ball out of my hand. I guess I became a big-mouthed catcher. I also learned how to be a catcher.

[Later in life, I always wanted to be catcher, as doing so placed one in position to see the entire action on the ball field. As an adult, I was catcher when my Little League team had batting practice because I could see how all the players were doing in the field and I could also be a "batting coach" right next to batters. I did graduate to a helmeted mask!]

As town baseball neared its end for the summer, I had a lot of "irons in the fire." I was driving as much as I could to hone my skills and also advertising to all the girls that there was a lover on the loose! I still had duties a Ross Grocery; I had worked out a "deal" where I would be able to go out for football and work on Saturdays and Sundays (football games were on Friday nights). I now made 50 cents an hour—big bucks; but the guys working Safeway were getting about a buck and a quarter. I worked for "slave labor," but I loved it and the folks there with whom I worked.

Driver's Ed was a dream come true for all teenagers, as it was the beginning of the road to driving the family's car! I passed the course and was on my way to driving without Mom or Dad in the front seat with me. I remember on my 16th birthday Dad let me drive Bruce somewhere by ourselves. I was cool! Then I came back to earth when I remembered that only two months earlier I had almost run over a chum of Bruce's. Dad was with me then and luckily Dad pulled the emergency brake just in time!

FOOTBALL GIVEN A TRY

Football was on the horizon for the oldest Cobb son whose brothers would one day both follow suit. I figured that being a school football player would raise my esteem and all I had to do was put on my equipment and uniform. Well, there was much more to it.

The team had to be at the gym at the high school in time to suit-up for summer practices and board a school bus for a ride two miles to edge-of-town baseball field where we practiced in the outfield grass. We worked out for two hours starting at 7:00AM and again in the evening at 5:00 PM. These were the dreaded routine "two-a-days" across America for most high school/college young men.

The worst thing was the heat across America at this time of the year, late August, and I was not ready for that new phenomenon with football. Oklahoma was known for blazing summer heat, so the temperature for the morning practice was above ninety degrees and one hundred and five at the beginning of practice in the afternoon. Add vigorous exercises and "head busting" turned on the sweat ducts a-flowing. Within the first fifteen minutes all the players would be soaked with sweat and that sweat load made bodies difficult to "cool" players' bodies. That was the name of the game, as coaches nation-wide had "learned" that the only way to get in shape, it required two hours of practice <u>without in-taking fluids</u>!

It was not unusual for two or three young football men in Oklahoma to die from heat injuries each summer. [This continued for about ten years when I played football, but it was easily solved. Very simple . . . drink fluids during strenuous exercise, even fluids like Gatorade. I watched a varsity college football team at practice in 1971 and players took a "drink break". The fare was actually, iced, Gatorade. Somebody got smart!]

As a newbie on the team, most of the equipment I was issued was old and battered. Our team had about 30 members and only about half of them got any new, modern equipment. In those days lightness was not found in most of our equipment, especially hip pads. Mine were big and bulky and made of thick cotton padding with a hard outside "shell," the better to protect one from big mean guys who wanted to hit you! But, as you sweated more and more the pads began heavier, so you were running around with an extra two or three pounds of sweat.

I was also issued a pair of football cleats. They were about two sizes too big for me and I had to use athletic tape wrapped around my left cleat to close up a gap between its upper shoe and its sole. [One can still see my tape job on my left in pictures!] I had to say, they worked okay.

My helmet was a hard plastic football helmet but it would never pass on a football player of today. It was heavy with plain heavy canvas rigging inside and no padding or foam protection. My helmet had a clear plastic face guard for protection, however, there was plenty of room for an adversary to slam his fist into my face. A few did that. Thanks, Corky; thanks Ron, thanks Jimmy. Good luck, young man! I would say I took a lot of hard knocks those two seasons. Funny, I enjoyed it.

I wore the same athletic support (jock strap), t-shirt, socks and practice jersey for about four practices before Mom washed it. Did it smell after those four practices? No, it smelled after the first practice!

Was I going to be cool quarterback, a bruising back or maybe a fleet end? Let's see. The coaches knew the talents of players from the previous years, but not us newbies. So, the coaches lined us up and had us run "wind sprints." The faster men became tries at offensive back or defensive backs and maybe an end. We slower ones became offensive/ defensive linemen. So, I became a guard (both ways).

The lighter linemen became guards; one was Jimmie Summer who was about 5' 11" and weighed 220# and paired with Charlie Bentz, about my size but tougher and with two years' experience. Corky Williams was the number three guard who saw a lot of game time and I was number four guard and I saw very little game experience but I saw plenty in practice, as I was always placed against Jimmie's 220 pounds. Our other varsity linemen, two tackles were Bill (chief) Ward a big Indian about 6' 3" and 250# and Ron Taylor (a class mate) at 5'11 and 170#. Of course, you guessed it. Bill Ward was tackle next to Jimmie against my side of line. Gulp, 470#!

The team head coach was Lester Jensen who had played at Oklahoma University and Oklahoma East Central and assistant Bill Dost who played at Tulsa University. Coach Jensen spent most of his time with the backs and Coach Dost the linemen. The coaches ran us through a lot of drills to toughen us up and "separate the men from the boys." I certainly started as a "boy," but eventually became a "big boy" as I learned what "it" was all about. I was used as a live blocking dummy for the others—the varsity; I was a "starter on the second team!" Those of us, the second team, had pride as more often than not we stopped the varsity team who were priming for our games. We worked this in late August and were ready for school to start at the end of twenty practices. We were obviously a better team than we started.

WATCH OUT ..... MUSCLE CRAMPS

One event really busted my butt and likely a few other butts. Hot August practice (two-a-day) for two hours each, no liquid intake, and forty yard wind sprints (4 or 5) at the end left one's body depleted of several fluids and juices that bodies craved. After showering back at the high school plenty of salt pills were available. Most other guys took three or four and I took one. Mistake! I made it home after the first morning practice and around one o'clock it hit me. My body was racked with muscle cramps: all the major and minor muscles in both my legs and shoulders cramped simultaneously. Those muscles were screaming for help and I was screaming for help from Mom because I had never felt such pain. I thought I surely might die!

Mom casually said, "Hey, you wanted to play football, not me!" I got it, but I was still hurting, really hurting. With water and salt the cramping stopped in about thirty minutes, but I can still remember that event and the pain. [To this day, I get muscle cramps if I am not ingesting salt.] After that episode I learned my lesson and was careful to manage my salt intake. Even though, I still had heat cramps, but not as bad as that first day's episode.

After the fourth two-a-day practice we had just about worn out the thin grass on the baseball field. So we were now playing football in our own Oklahoma "dust bowl." The "second team" got bashed, kicked in the ground with our helmet guards shoved in the piles of dry dirt, then arose to breathe the cloud of dust hovering over the playing area. Boy, was that ever fun!

I thought that I was doing what the coaches wanted—be a live blocking dummy and be there to give the varsity something to hit and not keep them from being successful with their plays. By the time I got to the middle of my senior year football season I realized it was too late—they really wanted me to tear their heads off. Wish Coach Dost had taking me aside in our first little dust bowl year and told me he wanted me to "tear people's heads off." Guess I did not have it in me.

In order to letter in football (achieve authority to wear a jacket or sweater with a "C") a player had to play at least one play per quarter and do that at least 16 times. You could be in one quarter and play sixteen plays, but that did not count, had to play in a least sixteen quarters. I got in about six or seven quarters but that was not enough. Naturally, about fifteen or so players like Buddy Wheeler and Bob Blackburn, my classmates, would play all quarters in the season, as they played both offensive and defense. We all wanted that "C," but one had to earn it!

After school started, we only had one practice a day after classes; practices lasted for about two and a half hours—still no fluid intake. We had to walk about three blocks from our locker room to Lantow Field next to the Claremont Elementary School. (The field was named after three Lantow football-playing brothers who were killed in WWII.) It was a nice grass field. Of course, we wore several of Lantow's grassy spots out over the season. We also had to walk or run back to the gym locker room. Many a football player would partake of neighborhood water faucets; "thank you madam."

We had a full ten games for the 1956 season. In addition to after class field practices, we also had thirty minute "chalk sessions" before school classes with the coaches to discuss what we did and did not do well at practices. We were becoming a pretty good football team and had good sized lineman and tough, quick backs and Doodle Woodson at quarterback. We won nine of our games and only lost, miserably, to Broken Arrow at their field, 0-31.

GETTING PSYCHED UP TO PLAY !!!

There was an event that really got to me emotionally. It was a pep rally in the school auditorium that seated about 325 students. The day for the first game and some later, the student body filed into the seats and clapped loudly to the songs played by the band as they were seated on the stage as were the cheer leaders (six young ladies; one of them was the pretty girl who lived next to me when we lived on 12th Street, Sharon Sheldon) in an attempt to raise the roof off the building. When everyone was in, the head coach led the football players down the aisle and seated them in the front rows. Little speeches were delivered and more noise was to be had. I was mesmerized! I had never felt like that as the noise and cheering and the whole student body was "lifting" me off the ground" to a higher plane emotionally. I loved it. I am sure all the football players were the same. I was ready to take on the whole team of every opposing football team. I was juiced!

Our first home game was with a small Catholic high school from Tulsa who we beat 33-6 which made us think we were something else! Heck, even I got in for a couple of plays. Of course, we of the second "varsity team" thought how tough we had made the real varsity team become so good. Broken Arrow slammed us back into reality, so the second varsity got to work on the first varsity and they won the last eight games of the 1956 season.

The Broken Arrow game was an away game and their field took vengeance upon me. Before the game we were all going through several drills to "warm up," as if we were not already warm. We linemen were doing our warm up drills in the end zone area that had a lot of chalk lines on the ground to make it attractive. As I went through our drills I felt a burning sensation on my right hip. I kept rubbing under my hip pads to relieve whatever was really burning the cheek of my right buttock. I thought that someone had dropped a lit cigarette down my hip pads. After our warm ups we went into the locker room for last pep talk. I took some water and doused it under my hip pads and that relieved the burning a bit. Later, I learned that evening the BA ground crew had used quick-lime marking on our end zone! (Quick-lime is not for marking fields but caustically clearing unwanted material.) I never learned if BA did that on purpose or just made a mistake! But they really lit my butt!

The quick-lime lit my butt, but BA football players lit the tails of our team in the 0-31 busting. Of course I had nothing to do with it, as you probably guessed few of our "second team varsity" got to play in the game. After beating that school from Tulsa 33-6 in our first game, we thought we were pretty hot stuff, but BA certainly taught us a lesson, "there are a lot of other teams that just might be better than you" (so you better get your stuff together at practice this week and improve a lot).

We did and "ran the table" (table pool term) of the remaining eight games in our schedule. We had a couple of really tough practices, the coaches made several adjustments, and the "second Varsity" made it extra tough on the first Varsity. Our coach had also had requests for us to play an extra game during Thanksgiving. We thought was neat but the coaches decided not as we had plenty to do without an additional game. We concluded the season with a 9-1 record. Surely, it was due to the sterling work of our second varsity team!

MR. JENSEN, MORE THAN FOOTBALL COACH

As football rolled on I had other needs to fulfil: school lessons, work at the grocery and attendance to requirements to seek an appointment to West Point. My junior year subjects were Algebra II, English, American Literature, American History and Chemistry. Of course, my math teacher was again the "OU linebacker of math" subjects and the head football coach, Mr. Jensen, was my teacher in American History. Once again I ended up with all A's for each of the four nine week periods. All A's for three whole years. And, Coach Jensen decided to send me to Oklahoma Central State College in Edmond one weekend in late April 1957 and compete in state competition for American History.

I vividly remember I had Mr. Jensen who taught our students (all juniors). Once a week he would write twenty questions on his chalk boards, tell us to read certain pages in our text book and be ready to cite the answers and meaning to the effect upon America and its citizens. I always enjoyed having his guidance, as we worked through the events and meanings for America as it worked itself into the greatness they achieved.

Bang! I won second place in the whole state! I could not wait until I got home to tell the coach that instead of having a 9-1 football team he had coached, he had also taught one of his students to win second place in American History in the whole state. I felt that for a guy who was in the education field primarily for athletics, then having one of his scholastic students to finish second in the state for his students was a real feather in his cap. (At least, I thought that was the way one would see it.) I think he was really pleased. Maybe he will make me the Varsity quarterback of this fall's team! Nah!

On one Sunday with nice weather, folks were headed to Claremore Lake for fun and fishing and eating and just lazing, and many would likely stop by Ross Grocery. The new owners wanted to go to church as they had been "big" in their church. They asked me if I could open the store at 8AM and stay until 12:30PM. I said sure, but Mom would have lunch for me at 12:30. No problem. Problem was that they did not return until about 2PM and between 12:30 and 2PM I swear I had over 50 customers, usually as many as 8 at the same time. And they did not just want a loaf of bread! I was swamped for at least two hours. The owners got here way late and just laughed. I went home to a late lunch and Mom was really mad at the owners. So is life!

IS COLLEGE OUT THERE FOR TYRUS, JR.?

Dad was hard at it lining up influential folks who would "rave" about me to US Congressional Senator Mike Monroney of Oklahoma. The key for an appointment to the US Military Academy was to convince the Senator that I was the best candidate from Oklahoma at that time. My thing was making good grades and be a leader by participating in a whole number of organizations. While I was not a great athlete I was there and working to help the team and maturing myself. I was heavy in things like the Math Club and the Science Club. I was President of the National Honor Society and math club. It did not "hurt" that I was second in the state in American History!

Dad used his outgoing personality to talk to mayors, police chiefs, doctors and state politicians. He asked a lot of folks to write to Senator Monroney about me. I knew that a few tests lay in front of me: first a test for the senator and if he picked me I would have to take the Military Academy tests for their approval for entry: medical, physical and then the SAT (Scholastic Aptitude Test) used to determine if one has enough "learning" to master the requirements of the academy. Dad never let up; nor did I.

Believe it was in February 1957 that I lost my job at Ross Grocery.

Was not my fault, but the owners sold the store to the Sumpter family, who had four daughters, and guess who became the store's clerks? Did not hurt badly. Dad was lining me up with a job working on a state highway maintenance crew. The crew chief was one of the men who Dad had gotten him to write a letter to the senator. When he heard about me, he said he would put me in to work during the summer of 1957.

Mom and Dad were good about letting me use the car especially on Saturday evenings which allowed me to run around with my friend, Paul Moore. We would hang at Teen Town and a lot of times we would go to Doctor's Melinder's home in the country just out of Claremore— hey, there were four girls there every Saturday, three of them were of the age Paul and I could mesh with: Marlene, Jeanie and Martha. Sometimes, we would drive way out in the sticks to the Ingersol ranch (about 20 miles) whose daughter went to Casia Catholic School in Tulsa with Marlene, and Paul was the Ingersol daughter's beau.

One Saturday night I was at Teen Town when Corky Williams, a teammate on the football team, came tearing into the dance floor and came over to me and out of the blue decked me (a sucker punch) to the floor. By the time I got up, the adult chaperones had Corky thrown out for the night. Wanda Dale and Charlotte Copp were right there and consoled me. I told everybody that I had no idea why he did that, but they did. It seems that Corky had just gotten ticketed by my Dad for speeding.

I never told my parents about the decking and there was no further action. See you on the football field.

Bruce and especially I loved to fly kites. One afternoon at our North Dorothy place I was flying a kite and I had over 2,500 feet of string on the kite and it got higher and higher. It was getting late and the kite was way up there and seemed to be steady, so I decided to stake the string to the ground and let it fly all night by itself. Next morning I was up early and ran out to see how the kite was doing. It was not "doing," and was down about three blocks from our house. The string was on houses, across a main road and was resting on the ground. Yes, I proved one thing – winds do die down when the night's winds abate.

When the Sumpter daughters moved in, I moved out. Then I knew what it meant to be "unemployed!" When school was out I was supposed to report to Herman Noland, the state highway department for Rogers County. Mr. Noland had known Dad for about three years as Dad patrolled the highways in the county and the very major highway was Route 66. However, I had an obligation to fulfill first and Mr. Nolan approved it. I had been selected to be a member of Oklahoma Boys' State sponsored by the American Legion. That was a real honor and helped me in seeking an appointment to West Point.

While at the Boys' State activities we attended classes to learn how state government worked and how officials were elected. We marched all over the place and at one afternoon activity was volleyball. I was on the front line when the ball came towards me, I jumped up to hit the ball back, but a teammate who was about a foot taller than me got the ball, and as he came down his elbow crashed into my nose. I was taken to the dispensary and the young medical student examined me and said my nose was broken, but the doctor on duty said "not broken." [Student was right and I dealt with it for 22 years.]

TO WORK ON THE ROAD, US 66

Dad made a deal (or asks a favor) with real nice man. Mr. Jim Foster, who was a "team boss" and was in charge of one of the maintenance trucks which was a five ton flatbed. He lived about four blocks from us, and after making my lunch, I walked to his house and got on the state truck that he parked at his house each night. Because of recent heavy rains that washed out embankments that demanded a lot of hours to fix, we worked 10 hour days, 5 days a week and occasionally 4 hours on Saturdays.

I was happy because that meant I was absolutely rich! I made $1.05 an hour, regular workers made $1.10 an hour and truck-driving team-bosses made $1.15 an hour. Such were state highway employees in those days.

Mr. Herman Nolan, the state's county supervisor, had three truck-driving teams and Jim's area was assigned to US 66. At times all teams joined together on big jobs. On Jim's team were two other fellows who were in their late forties and two summer hires, me and Donnie Woodson, who was two years older than I. I knew Donnie from high school; he was on the football team. We got along famously and we spent the whole summer riding on the back bed of our truck. I will admit, Donnie and I were the hardest workers. Not too many guys are going to work very hard for $1.10 an hour!

Folks, working on Oklahoma highways in the summer were in a rather "warm" place to be. Temperature there approached 120 degrees with a blazing sun. Remember one week that our team was assigned to unload train gondola cars that were loaded with pavement repair material, a mixture of dirt, chat, and thick oil, we called it "patch." Seven train gondola cars were delivered to a train siding in the Claremore rail yard about half a mile from the highway department yard.

One state man was a heavy equipment operator who drove a road grader and a "steam shovel" that had a large two jawed bucket that opened, moved into a gondola, scooped up a load of patch, swung out of the gondola with the load of patch and deposited it onto the back of our trucks. Then the patch was dumped in our work yard. When finished, we had enough patch to last about six months of repairing road holes, large and small.

Donnie and I spent a week of working in the gondolas with hand shovels to set up batches of patch for the steam shovel operator to scoop and swing onto the awaiting trucks.

In the mid-fifties very few automobiles had air conditions. One state highway patrolman stopped a New York state car speeding on Route 66 that summer. When he approached the car, he observed the occupants were four bare-breasted women! Obviously, the patrolman was a bit taken-a-backed but knowing how hot it was he told them they must slow down a little. And, he did not issue a ticket!

Donnie and I, working on the back of the truck, could see into cars as they sped by, but we never saw those four shirtless ladies again. And we were watching!

Twice I had to be taken home from the highway, as I had heat stroke with dizzy spells and threw up. I had a terrible feeling and felt like I was dying. Mom's attention solved my pains in a couple of hours, and I returned to work the next day.

As the summer moved along and my bank account rose with my 50 dollars a week was stashed in my savings account. And all along Dad was at work lining up folks' letters for Senator Monroney. And football two-a-day practices were waiting to gear up.

Our state highway crew was always on a lookout for things of value. We always collected a lot of glass soda pop bottles, as cans and plastic bottles were not yet on the market. We would collect them and use them to buy sodas when we had enough; they were worth 2 cents each. Another thing we always looked for were good tires that might have fallen off trucks on the road. One time I spotted one such truck wheel/tire on side the highway. We all examined the wheel/tire. It was in good shape and a couple of the old timers knew a place where the owner might buy it from us (me). We took it there at a filling station on Route 66 and the guy payed us $20; I got $5 and the other four guy split the rest. Good money for sodas!

Donnie and I were masters of the straight-nosed shovels up on the truck bed breaking up the patch for the guys on the road for repairing holes. At other times we worked on jack-hammers to break up concrete that set up wrong when contracted crews had laid out poured concrete. The summer passed quickly as we worked and joked with everybody included the older fellows. One of the older guys was a Silver Star veteran of WWII and had been wounded that left his voice interrupted and he had to work hard to voice out words. But he was funny and he did not mind that we called him "Whispering Jack!"

Senior class awaited me.

A ZEBRA SENIOR

Before senior classes started, we of the football team had other duties. Onto the grass of the baseball field's outfield – soon to become our little dust bowl – we went. Last year our team had a sterling season, except for that drubbing by Broken Arrow, 0-31. Once again we would face Broken Arrow in our second game of the season, but this time at home. So, we had better get to work!

We had lost our two biggest linemen to graduation so the coaches had to rebuild the team. We had a pretty good quarterback, Monk Hall, and a whole bunch of running backs with good size. As expecting, the Zebras still ran an OU spilt-T formation that nearly every high school in the state ran. Line splits were easy: guard 6 inches from the center; tackle 1 foot from the guard; end 1 yard from the tackle. Hard to forget that. Occasionally, one end split about 3-4 yards. Of course, our setup always meant the eleven opposing guys were right on top of us.

Two-a-days were no different than last year. Blazing sun, scorching temperatures, and no water. I made it to the #3 guard, as Charles Bentz remained in his slot and Corky Williams took Jimmie Summers' position.

Monk (Kenneth Hall) steered the crew of big running backs that would become the strength of our team. I was now a member of the senior horde. We always had enough cars, so after each two-a-day we headed to the Stewart's Root Beer stand on the OMA hill (Oklahoma

Military College; 9th thru junior college; many an OMA guy, especially the 'college guy', 'stole' our girls away!). Back to drinking root beer and attacking ice cream. The money I had earned that summer from the state really came in handy.

Senior year handed me another batch of courses: Solid Geometry, English, Spanish, English Literature, Physics and Typing I. I only took Typing for first semester, as I just wanted to learn the keyboard; I did. Hopefully some more A's were waiting for me. My junior year scholastically I was honored by being selecting into the HS National Honor Society (NHS); then, I was elected as President of the high school's NHS and Math Club my senior.

Our first football game was a downer, as we were defeated 0-19 by Tahlequah. Surely, the coaches did not expect that. I thought this looked like this season is doomed and doubt if I will ever wear a letter jacket. Some extra tough practices this week.

BROKEN ARROW (HOME) GAME

A couple of possessions of the ball and someone hollered, "Corky has been hurt!" Then "Ty go in for Corky." Corky was not hurt real badly, but our coaches said he was out of the game. The player opposite me was a submarining defensive player and all he did for the whole game was dive under me. I got it! On every play I buried him and he never got a tackle in the game nor did he mess up any of our plays. I told the coach and Monk, our quarterback, that he could run any play through me and that guy could not stop anybody. It worked! In the third quarter we were on the Broken Arrow five yard line and Monk called for the fullback, Charlie Battenfield, to run directly through my hole. He shot straight into the end zone for a touchdown, and I got my picture in the Sunday paper standing in the background watching Charlie go in. I was on the first Varsity for the rest of the game and we beat Broken Arrow

20-0. I was on cloud nine and waltzed into the Copp's Café downtown for a piece of pie and a cup of coffee.

The next Monday at practice Coach Dost, the line coach, said, "what were you doing standing up in that picture like you had nothing to do?" "Hey, coach you did not see my man did you; he was flat on the dirt at my feet!" Coach Dost got a kick out of my retort. Corky was okay and he was back at his position and I was back to #3 guard.

We played seven more games and ended up with a 6-3 record. I did play in a few quarters but I did not make the 16 quarters to letter, think I had about eight or nine. When the season was over Coach Jensen called me in and say I played enough to letter because there was a clause in the rules: if a player made a significant contribution to the team one could letter. My feat in the Broken Arrow game was a "significant contribution." I lettered!

THERE'S MORE THAN FOOTBALL

I had been dating a young girl, Jeannie Rogers, for a while. She was really cute and was mature for her age (about three years younger than me) but Mom decided she was too young for me. I was upset, but I chased some other girls and snuck around to take Jeannie out kissing!

Another girl, a class behind me was one of the most popular girls in the school, Hoytanna Lessley. I told one of my football classmates, Ronald Taylor, I was taking her out. He told me that whatever I did, absolutely do not try to French kiss her, as she will go crazy. Well, we parked at Claremore Lake and I tried to kiss her, but she held her mouth open. That was a signal for French kissing, but Ronald told me to do not even try that. So, I did not. Duh. [I told Ronald about that 25 years later at a reunion and he denied it, but something like that I still remember it because that young lady probably told all the girls in school!]

I still fondly remember Nancy Galbraith because I was smitten the first time I saw her my freshman year at the little grocery by Claremont Elementary. I dated her several times and she was always nice, but I began to realize the competition with older young men and OMA hill cadets were just too stiff. She was a young lady who got nicer and more beautiful each time I saw her.

GO TO TULSA

I was notified in the fall of 1957 to report to a Post Office in Tulsa to take a Civil Test for Senator Monroney to see if all the folks supporting me for West Point really knew the truth about me. Doing well on that test would help the Senator make his decision about me and several other young men testing. One Saturday I went to Tulsa and took the four hour test. I felt good about it, but you never know. Now, just wait!

Even though I still had several hundred dollars in my savings account from my state summer work, I went looking for a job right after football season. Claremore had two dry goods stores, J.C. Penney's and C.R. Anthony's on Main Street about 40 feet apart. My family had purchased clothing from both stores (I remember buying my "white sports coat" {like Marty Robins} from Penney's my junior year for the prom; I used it for my proms, as did brothers, Bruce and Teddy; great buy!) After interviewing, I was hired by Mr. Charlie Cunningham, manager of C.R. Anthony's.

I was to work after school for two hours each day and all day on Saturday. After school, I swept the entire store, both floors and on Wednesday I washed the outdoor show case windows. On Saturdays in shirt and tie I was a sales person in the men's section plus the shoe section. I did fine and had one embarrassing incident.

One Saturday about 2PM, I was working the floor and had to relieve myself. Place not crowded, so I went in the back to the restroom. As I was relieving myself I thought I was through too quickly and emptied about a third of my urine went down the front of my pants. I tried to dry my pants, but no luck, and I had to get back on the floor. I did and quickly headed for the radiator and straddled it to try to dry by pants. Did not work, and a lady and her daughter came up to me and asked for help. Gulp; double gulp! I helped them and they did not say anything, but I was melting inside!

I was notified by Senator Monroney's office to report to Ft. Sill to take West Point entrant tests: medical, physical, and scholastic. I had met another guy who took the civil test earlier in Tulsa and he was also notified to Ft. Sill. My dad hooked up with his parents and Dad took us both to Ft. Sill. We got as far as Marlowe, OK about 25 miles from Ft. Sill when we got in a heavy snow storm. New plan! Dad dropped us at Marlowe's dime store which was also the bus stop. Dad felt he should go back and we were to catch the bus for Ft. Sill as it would do better in the snow.

My friend and I missed the bus to Ft. Sill because we spent too much talking to a cute (big breasted also) young sales-girl at the dime store. Was not me; the other guy! We caught a later bus and had more time to talk.

In April 1958, the state education folks were once again administering tests on many high school subjects that was done each year; same tests that I won second place in American History. This time my "linebacker" math teacher, Miss Gassett, was entering me in the math test; two of her former students had placed in this exam in the top three in 1955 and 1956. Here I am and by "crackey" I won second place. I felt great because Miss Gassett had done it again!

In May, I was notified that I had to go to Tinker Field in Del City, as I had high blood pressure at the Ft. Sill medical examination. I would have to have my blood pressure (BP) taken once in the morning and once in the afternoon three days in a row. Dad took me, and we stayed at Aunt Etha's home in OKC. I did not do well the first day and Dad talked to a young Air Force medical first lieutenant asked him to help as college meant this and he (me) was so nervous that that surely made BP higher than normal. Next two days the 1LT let me lay down a couple of minutes before taking my BP. Final BP got just under what was necessary to "pass." [Since then I "suffer" from what is called "white coat tension." When I see someone about to take my BP it goes up automatically.]

I was notified just before graduation that I was going to West Point as a plebe (freshman)! Thank you, Senator Monroney!

Folks, time to get my white sports coat out and get ready for the Senior Prom. Jan Rogers, a junior, agreed to be my date. Jan was nice looking and rather shapely as I recall. It was a prom as most proms so we got bored and most people left around 10:30 PM. One of my classmates, Hays Gilstrap, said that we could go to his family's cabin on Lake Eucha and have a party! If my Mom and Dad had known what we were up to they would had roped me and tied me down. The lake was about 65 miles away and it was night and it was one-way roads. Fortunately, I had been there a couple of times before, but not driving the car, at night and with somebody's daughter.

No problem! Really became no big deal. But, . . . no music, no eats, no kissing place. Let's go home. Off we headed for Claremore about midnight and I got Jan home at 1:30 AM. Parents never knew where we had been. Sneaky. Kids!

Now it was time for the last nine weeks quarter finals of which I had never taken finals because of my many A's and perfect attendance. But this time I was out of classes when I spent four days at Tinker Field to retest my blood pressure. So, I had to take all of my finals. I did but had a sinking feeling as I did not well on one final and got a B. I still came out as one of three Valedictorians because the last 9-weeks final did not count for honors. Do not know what Glenda Huneke and Nancy

Whitenton made on their finals, but those two ladies and I were dubbed Valedictorians!

Dad took me around to some of the kind folks who had written letters to Senator Monroney recommending me as an appointee to West Point. Several of the folks actually gave me money as a high school graduation present. I remember hundred dollar bills from Doctor Melinder and Doctor Khour'I, our dentist in Chelsea.

As I put my early years to print (I hope) I must re-visit Coaches Jensen and Yost who were instrumental in maturing me towards manhood. I was not one of their most talented of football players, but they gave me something few can. That is mature toughness to be able to successfully overcome things and events that tend to push one away from goals assigned. Gentlemen, I pray you can "hear" me, "thank you, I love to have known you and served you."

On my 18ᵗʰ birthday Dad was taken me around and we had lunch. He said I had to have a beer as I was 18 now! I did and did not like the beer. Couple of years later, I sort of liked a couple of beers! Guess my body "aged with time!"

I had met a couple of the OMA hill cadets when we were at Ft. Sill to take the battery of West Point tests, Mike Jones and Tom Murray, both from OKC area. Mike's father had died so his mom was working and alone. My Mom (had worked as a secretary at OMA for a couple of years) and Dad hooked up with the Jones' and my parents were happy to get the boys on an airplane in the OKC airport for New York City.

Mike and I hooked up, from which girlfriends we were leavin, for a "kissing place" at Lake Claremore the night before we were heading to Oklahoma City. Mike had a steady girl from Claremore, Doris Lunsford, he had dated for a while, and me with Jeannie Rogers. Ladies, nice way to say bye-bye!

The next day in OKC, I vividly remember my Mom longingly

watching our plane on Braniff International Airways, whose hub was Will Rogers World (there's that name again!) airport, taxi for takeoff.

Stopped in St. Louis and finished in NYC. Stayed overnight, saw a new, epic movie, "Ben Hur," starring Charlton Heston, in New York City's Times Square.

Next morning, 1 July 1958, we were on a bus out of Port Authority Bus Terminal and in one hour we drove through the gate at West Point and up to the barracks. I, gulped, and I knew my childhood was absolutely over.

Oh, my God, what has this young Okie gotten into!

Printed in the United States
by Baker & Taylor Publisher Services